My wild field catalogue of flowers
Grows in my rhymes as thick as showers
Tedious and long as they may be
To some, they never weary me
The wood and mead and field of grain
I could hunt oer and oer again
And talk to every blossom wild
Fond as a parent to a child

John Clare

About the author

Pete Stroh is an accidental botanist who has worked professionally in the field of natural history for the past 25 years. He is the author of numerous scientific papers, is a regular contributor to *British Wildlife* magazine, and has published several books about the flora of our Isles, including *Grassland plants of the British and Irish lowlands*, *Threatened Plants in Britain & Ireland*, and *Plant Atlas 2020*.

Originally hailing from south Devon, he has been based in the north of Northamptonshire since the turn of the century following a largely bohemian existence in Scotland for much of the 1990s, when amongst other things he worked in a record shop, ventured up munros, frequented late-night bakeries, and lived for a time with ospreys.

The Cuckoo
Calls the Year

Dedication

For Lizzy, Eva, Iris, Bramble

The Cuckoo Calls the Year

*An appreciation of plants, birds
and other wildlife living close to home*

Pete Stroh

MERLIN UNWIN BOOKS

First published in Great Britain by Merlin Unwin Books Ltd 2025

Merlin Unwin Books
6 Rural Enterprise Centre
Eco Park Road
Ludlow
SY8 1FF
UK

www.merlinunwin.co.uk
The author asserts their moral right to be identified with this work.

ISBN 978 1 913159 82 5
Typeset in 12 pt Adobe Caslon Pro by Joanne Dovey, Merlin Unwin Books
Printed by Bell & Bain Ltd, UK

 Carry Akroyd is a painter and printmaker living in
Northamptonshire. Usually her subject is the unspectacular
arable farming landscape with its marginal wildlife. She has
illustrated several books, and has had three compilations of
her own work published. www.carryakroyd.co.uk

Connections

My formative years, from the ages of two to seven, were spent on the other side of the world, in the North Island of 1970s New Zealand. We had a large garden to explore – at least it seemed so at the time – and I soon became fascinated with insects, grasshoppers in particular. Some of my earliest memories are of running around barefoot in the garden with a 'bug catcher', a toy with a long handle and a clear plastic globe that could be snapped open and shut using a simple trigger mechanism. Once grasshoppers were caught within the globe, I would admire them as they attempted desperately to escape their prison, springing upwards, turning somersaults, bashing against an invisible forcefield. I didn't decapitate or pull the legs off the creatures I detained and such sensibilities are perhaps one of the reasons why I am not now an entomologist. Instead, I would try to transfer them from the globe to my cupped palms, and when successful, feel their exoskeletons knocking against soft skin until they were still. It was then possible, for a brief moment, to open my hands and examine the wonderful colours and patterns adorning legs and head and thorax before they cottoned on to the fact that freedom was no longer restricted. I remember vividly trying this technique with a wasp, at a time when I was blissfully ignorant of their reputation. I did not attempt it a second time.

Caterpillars were also fair game and not nearly as mobile. The monarch butterfly's chunky larvae, spectacular creatures with long black antennae and a zebra-striped body interconnected with lime-green sections, were easy to find as they munched on leaves in the garden. They soon became my obsession. I hand-picked and housed the caterpillars in an old glass tank with wire mesh fixed across the top. After multiple fatalities and a bit of research by my mum,[1] it was clear that in order for them to survive I would need to find and feed them leaves from their foodplant, milkweed,[2] rather than the random diet I had selected which consisted mainly of grass clippings. This meant that I had to identify and find a specific species of plant; with hindsight, this was a revelation. It had not occurred to me that one plant was very different from another, let alone that one species might depend on another for survival.

Milkweed was a good first plant to learn. Not only is it a statuesque species with obvious drooping clusters of beautiful white flowers and wonderfully

---

[1] I couldn't yet read to a high enough standard – to be fair, I was only four years old

[2] Specifically, the plant in our garden was *Gomphocarpus fruticosus*

plump hairy pods that burst open to reveal a mass of cottony seeds, milkweed also contains a secret weapon that the caterpillar harnesses for protection. The plant produces sap when attacked which is then ingested by the caterpillar, causing it no harm but making such a potentially tasty, plump morsel toxic to predators; as well as being curiously beautiful, I learnt that the caterpillar was clever too. The milkweed leaves kept the captives alive and in those pre-internet days (indeed, our black and white television had only one channel) I spent hours watching them methodically devouring their food one thin strip at a time, heads moving in a rhythmic motion from the edge of the leaf to the central vein, until one half was consumed and the caterpillar turned to repeat its hypnotic technique on the remaining half.

As the weeks went by, I became increasingly attached to the caterpillars and so was devastated when they started to vanish. I can't recall exactly when I noticed the appearance of shiny jade pods dangling from the wire mesh but I do remember being told that each pod, known as a chrysalis, was made by the caterpillar and that it was now inside turning itself into a butterfly. I thought the explanation both confusing and deeply unfair. My disappointment started to evaporate, however, and levels of excitement surge when each chrysalis began to turn first a black colour and then semi-transparent, revealing the smudge of a creature inside that was certainly not the pet I had raised. I will always remember walking home from kindergarten, in pain after stubbing a big toe, an event which happened regularly due to my strong objection to wearing footwear, to find in the glass tank a dark wet creature slowly emerging from its changing room. It hung upside down, long black legs clasped to the remains of the abandoned transparent husk, a strange curled 'tongue' protruding, wings stunted but beginning to take shape, expanding, slowly revealing an impossibly fresh bright orange and black with pure white polka dots. Drying out after rebirth, the butterfly was motionless save for the twitching of its wings as meconium (a sort of waste liquid left over from the chrysalis stage) pumped through its veins, and I made the most of this time to appreciate every detail of what to this day still seems to be such a miraculous transformation. As the days went by, more butterflies emerged and I began to name each one. Largely as a result of my fondness for them, some eventually died in the aquarium, but I was coerced into releasing the last few, standing open-mouthed on the lawn as they sped over the tin roof of our house, creatures that I had found as fat, earthbound caterpillars metamorphosed into butterflies set free to repeat a life cycle perfected over 50 million years.

Perhaps in another life the spectacular peacock butterfly, a common species of English gardens whose black caterpillars mass together to spin silk webs where nettles are left to grow, would have been my gateway drug into the natural world. Or I might have disturbed a nest of yellow meadow ants and become hooked on their apparently random movements, which I would later learn to be complex, communal interactions. Or it could have been a fantastically colourful orange slug skulking slowly across the patio, or a pungent stinkhorn fungus emerging in nearby woods, a goldcrest spotted feeding on teasel seed heads, or the fleeting sighting of a hare in full flight. Alternatively, it might have taken until adulthood to become aware of the astonishing array of different lifeforms that are hidden in plain sight and continue to persist, despite all that is thrown at them. I hope that at some point I would have appreciated that we are a part of the natural world, not separate from it. You don't have to be an expert botanist to admire the majesty of an oak tree, just as you don't need to be a master stonemason to appreciate the grandeur of a medieval church, or a skilled musician to be moved by a Bach cantata. Discovering what grows and hunts and flies and sings within walking distance of your home is an experience which costs nothing but has the potential to enhance your life, and change our world.

Rules for writing

I chose at the outset to restrict my wanderings to within the boundaries of the parish where I live ('my patch'), and to try to write at least once a week, for one year. As providence would have it the first day of writing in early spring coincided with hearing my first cuckoo of the year, and so I decided to end my observations when a cuckoo returned the following spring. This meant that the book actually covers a year and three days – not bad timekeeping, all things considered, for a bird that had to travel back from the Congo basin.

There were two other rules that I attempted to follow. The first, which I kept to, was to write about events as I witnessed them. I chose to use my phone for this purpose and so had to ensure that the device was fully charged before heading out. I could have used a pencil and paper, but notes on the phone can be cut and pasted into a document without the need to transcribe from hastily scribbled hieroglyphs. I resisted venturing outdoors if it was raining – writing on a small wet screen is a skill that I have yet to master – although the 'accuracy' of the weather forecast has resulted in me now knowing many excellent spots to shelter from a deluge.

The second rule was more challenging, and involved discarding any negative baggage. This statement requires a brief explanation. After working as a botanist for more than 20 years, walking the countryside had almost imperceptibly turned into a disheartening endeavour. I would rest at a viewpoint and contemplate how much better it would be if a pasture had not been drenched with herbicide, if a woodland had not been planted up with regimented lines of conifer crops, if an arable field could every so often not be ploughed right up to the bloody roots of the hedgerow. I walked along species-poor road verges knowing that a simple change in the cutting regime could lead to a more diverse, floriferous scene. I crossed meadows that were gradually losing their key species, aware that even slightly higher numbers of grazing cattle and sheep would make all the difference. As Mark Twain might have commented, being outdoors with a jaded ecologist is a good walk spoiled. I fell into the mindset of seeing what was missing, increasingly blind to what was present. And I came to the realisation that I needed to reset, to appreciate nature as I once had.

Many have written about our increasing disconnection with the natural world and the consequences of such detachment. As we lose nature as a part of our identity, it becomes less relevant, less valued, and so more easily discarded. At the same time, we are pummelled by stories of loss and decline, of a landscape gradually stripped of life. One might sometimes wonder if there is anything left to appreciate, conserve or restore, even if we could find a way to reconnect. I decided that for my writing I would restrict grumblings to a minimum, to observe rather than judge. This took a bit of getting used to but proved ultimately to be a liberating and at times unexpectedly meditative experience.

A brief introduction to my patch

A parish is defined simply as a village which has its own church. As it happens, our village contains two: the first dating to the 12th century with a spire that casts its shadow over a central green, and the second built in the late 13th century, towering over surrounding fields and situated at the southern limits of habitation. Consequently, the village was, for 600 years or so, divided into two separate parishes until they were merged in the 19th century. This 'modern' fused boundary encompasses a relatively large area, covering 1,200 hectares that fits within a shape that, with a bit of imagination, resembles a valiant attempt to draw the British coastline from memory (although we are about as far away from the sea as it is possible to be).

On the highest ground[3] marking the western parish boundary there is a thick mixture of ancient and coniferous woodland. A descent eastward from this viewpoint passes large arable fields, pastures and a circuitous green lane, eventually reaching a plateau housing about 340 souls. The land then continues a gently sloping downward trajectory over more arable and pasture, to wet woodland and water meadows, until finally coming to rest by a

---

[3] Rising to just 80m above sea level, so not that high

wide river, curving in a giant oxbow to define the eastern and southern boundaries. The large nook of land formed by this bend in the river has twice been transformed radically in recent times: first from a tranquil pasture to an industrial scene as aggregates were dug out for the construction of roads, and then, once the resource had been exhausted, transfiguring into flooded 'gravel pits' as giant craters filled with water, aquatic and liminal life, wildfowl and waders. A scene of devastation 60 years ago is now protected as a Site of Special Scientific Interest.

The northern limits of the parish are marked by a grand 15th century manor house and an unfinished Elizabethan lodge in the shape of a Greek cross. In the spaces in between there are ditches, brooks, snaking footpaths, miles of interlocking hedgerow, a couple of minor roads. You might drive past and think it to be a pretty place, albeit rather uniform, with no rugged hills or mountains to frame the scene, nothing particularly special. We shall see.

19th April

It is a warm, still day. Orange-tip and brimstone butterflies, flowering cowslips, daisies, deadnettles and dandelions, buff and red-tailed bumblebees, beetles mating precariously in mid-air, birdsong and the buzzing of flies accompany me up to the ancient woodland. Paths that were quagmires a few weeks ago are now solid underfoot.

I approach the wood following the public footpath that rises up and along the far western boundary of the village, rather than taking the more direct route that enters the wood at its southern edge. This diversion means that I will amble in a large, anti-clockwise loop, with the vague intention of checking a large pond for tadpoles near to the end of the walk. This way also provides a gentler transition from farmland to woodland, with pastures instead of arable fields leading to the brow of a hill, past magnificent oaks and the rose-pink buds of wild crab apple, their sweet-scented flowers a magnet for honeybees. As the path opens up to reveal tidy green fields contrasting with a wild wooded boundary, a farmer on his quad bike motors past, towing a wooden crate filled with lambs, delivering them from the farm in the distance where they were born a couple of weeks ago. When the farmer reaches the middle of the field he dismounts, the engine still running, and opens the back of the crate, releasing skittering bodies still to fill out and put into proportion long gambolling legs. Their first experience of the outdoors is a field at the top of the world.

The woodland ground flora is dotted with dog violets. Many of their flowers are still concertinaed and so hard to spot, on the cusp of unfurling, sharing spaces with ground ivy and lesser celandine under a canopy of dog's mercury. Speckled wood butterflies with fresh chocolate-brown and yellow patterned wings bask on bramble leaves and buttercream primroses. Bee-flies, the micro teddy bears of the fly world, hover and dart in rapid staccato motions around the first flowering bluebells that rise above broad wild garlic leaves. The bee-flies are joined by hoverflies and wasps of a variety of species and dimensions, from the size of a pinhead to the length of a fingernail.[4]

The vast majority of garlic plants are in bud, but a few on a south-facing woodbank are in full bloom, the two large papery bracts that recently enveloped pointed buds falling away to reveal a mass of white flowers held on long thin pedicels. The slightest crunch of a leaf releases a powerful garlic scent, and the woodland floor is in places awash with them. Many of the oaks that tower

---

[4] It might surprise you to learn that there are around 9,000 species of wasp in the UK. Almost all of these are 'solitary' wasps and most look very different to the black-and-yellow striped 'social' wasps that live together in nests and keep us company on picnics.

above are peppered with white splodges of a lichen, some covered to such an extent that it looks as if paintballers have been using them for target practice. I clamber over the trunk of a thick, twisted sallow resting over a muddy ditch full of the impressions of fallow deer, emerge onto a sunny ride, more or less where I thought I would be, and make my way to the destination pond, hoverflies at head height leading the way. There has been little rain for a month or more, but still the levels of the pond are much lower than I expected, a thick brown ring separating the grassy edge from the mirrored surface. Predatory boatmen row back and forth while whirligig beetles move erratically over the water, wing casings lit by the sun and appearing like droplets of mercury. No frogspawn, though.

Great tits nesting nearby make clear their annoyance at me being here, insistent alarm calls moving through the branches. As I sit and watch the beetles navigate their complex maze, chasing in and out of water starworts, floating sweet-grass and duckweed, a loud clear call comes from the tall pines, budded oaks and fractured turquoise sky, finding its way past the spaces between stout trunks, brambles, willow and blackthorn. It takes a second or two for the sound to register. It is a lost sound, conjuring images of sandals and shorts and flower-strewn meadows, of sweet scents and light evenings, abundance and diversity. Six clear hiccoughing notes skim perfectly across the surface of the water to meet me.

A cuckoo is calling.

The Cuckoo (Part I)

Harbinger of spring and fertility, a loathsome parasite, unfaithful companion, a master of deception: the cuckoo has a complicated reputation in folklore woven by myth, legend and observation. The call of the first cuckoo, materialising out of a background of familiar and well-worn winter sound, is to me an unfailingly joyous refrain. The birds that continue to return each year have undertaken an extraordinary round trip since departing last July, travelling from our meadows and woodlands southwest via Spain and Morocco, crossing the vast expanse of the Sahara Desert, finally alighting in the warm, humid climes of the Congo basin.

Our cuckoo[5] is about the same size as a well-fed, slightly stretched-out pigeon. Its upper parts are a blue-grey colour, its head and chest are white with dark barring, its tail is long and its wings are pointed at the tips. Whilst the cuckoo's return has been welcomed as the herald of spring for generations, their arrival has darker undertones for birds such as the reed warbler and the dunnock. For the cuckoo is as famous for its behaviour as it is for its song.

22nd April

Ash flowers are erupting from bluntly pointed black buds, releasing yellow clouds of pollen when brushed with a hand, or by the wind. Ash is classified as a dioecious species, that is to say an individual tree is either male or female. Those with flowers holding a mass of purple-red anthers resembling clusters of plump raspberries are the

---

[5] There are 54 cuckoo species globally

males; the splayed female flowers bear only pistils[6] and are reminiscent of loose bushels of slender broccoli spears on the turn. But the ash's sexual orientation is not quite as clear-cut as some books suggest. Whilst it is true that some trees in the village are either one sex or the other, in fact a closer look at others in flower shows that the gender of a tree is often expressed as a continuum, with both male and female flowers present. In other words, such trees are not strictly dioecious, but rather monoecious. And rather remarkably, it is possible, over time, for ash trees to change their sexual function from predominantly male to female, and vice versa, exhibiting a kind of gender fluidity that would seem very 21st century, but happens in the natural world more often than you might imagine.

25th April

After a leisurely stroll down to the river in the fading early evening light, I am almost in sight of home when I notice a small something stumbling through the grass ahead of me, close to a fallen ash limb by the edge of the pasture. I raise my binoculars through which I have recently watched lapwings displaying over water meadows, and am astonished to find that I am staring at a fox cub, perhaps only a couple of weeks old and most likely out on its first adventure. Its head turns to stare in my direction and I stand as still as I can, but it doesn't seem to mind my presence, if it sees me at all. Although foxes have become a fairly common sight in urban areas, with many seemingly having lost their instinctive fear of humans, country foxes are far

---

[6] Pistils are comprised of the stigma, style, and ovary

more skittish for obvious reasons. I walk as close as I
dare with exaggerated slowness until there is no need
for binoculars. A second cub emerges from behind
the broken ash and they both proceed to clamber over
fallen branches and among the tussocky grass in front
of me as I watch, transfixed, their pale grey-orange
bodies occasionally lost from sight before heads and
black-tipped tails emerge where the grass is shorter. It
is a thrilling and completely unexpected experience in a
field that I have walked perhaps a thousand times.

I watch the cubs play until they become dark-grey
blobs barely distinguishable from the surrounding
vegetation, then take a circuitous route back home,
trying my best to not disturb them. I plan to return later
in the week, although I know that the next encounter,
if it happens, will be very different, arriving with a
sense of expectation rather than the unique thrill of
a chance encounter. I have only seen fox cubs playing
once before, a long time ago when wandering in an
ancient dwarf-oak woodland in the Scottish Borders,
after rising too early in a tent pitched next to a narrow,
gin-clear brook. The images from that morning are
still as sharp in my memory today as they were when
imprinted over thirty years ago and if I make it to
another thirty years, I'm certain that today's encounter
will remain just as vivid.[7]

---

[7] I caught sight of the fox cubs a few weeks later by a stone wall that
divides the pasture from a field of young barley. They were pouncing
into deep grass, perhaps playing but more likely practising hunting
techniques. Their coats were a deep orange, much more fox-like in
colour. The encounter lasted a few seconds before they got wind of me,
their senses sharpened, innocence lost.

29th April

It is early morning at the gravel pits and I'm half-asleep, walking on autopilot as the dog leads the way. Patches of gold pockmark the small nature reserve on the other side of the brook, marsh marigolds glowing against the fawn and dull orange tones of last year's rushes. Pastures that border the water of the largest pit have a generous scattering of cowslips. A couple of cuckoos call in the distance, plotting their deception while warblers sing out in the scrubby margins, staking out their territories.

As I turn for home, a deep note reverberates from the reeds nearby, as if someone or something with enviable lung capacity is blowing over the top of a very large, empty bottle. I have to wait for a second and third note to be sure that I haven't imagined it. It is a sound that your body feels almost as keenly as your ears hear. In twenty years, I have been fortunate on a couple of occasions to see this creature skulking about in reeds during the winter months, but this is different. There are a few sounds in the world of nature conservation that can be said to be 'iconic', and the booming bittern is surely one of them. It represents so much more than a potential breeding territory for one of our rarest birds. These rather plump, beautiful herons with pale, buff-brown plumage adorned with dark streaks and bars were once a fairly common bird of our lowland wetlands but were also, unfortunately for them, rather tasty and a favourite on the menu of posh medieval banquets. By the turn of the 20th century bitterns were on the brink of extinction, their numbers depleted first by hunting and later exacerbated by the widespread drainage and destruction of their habitat. In 1997, only eleven booming bitterns were recorded across the entirety of the UK. Since then, the situation has been turned around through a combination of research, reedbed creation, management to maintain suitable conditions, the skill and expertise of conservationists, and a lot of money, much of which was provided by European coffers. There are now approaching 200 booming birds, and it is not a little ironic that the male bird that I hear calling is attempting to set up home in an area that sixty years ago was a very large hole in the ground, water constantly being pumped out whilst the land was gradually exhausted of aggregates.

The decision to let this landscape revert to water and wilderness, instead of returning to farmland, was one ahead of its time, and we are now reaping the benefits of such foresight. But not in their wildest dreams would the planning authorities have imagined booming bitterns naturally colonising the area. Proof, if it were needed, that nature can recover if we are willing to give it enough space, and a helping hand.

2nd May

On the north-eastern edge of the village, placed precariously at the margins of an eroding bank that slides down to a shallow brook, the flowers of marsh marigold rise up on thick green stalks, shining golden petals reflecting light filtered through fresh green blackthorn leaves. Having seen their colour from a distance a few days ago, I'm now able to admire their form nose-to-petal. Although the kingcup, as it is otherwise fondly known, has become less common in the English lowlands in recent times, it is a tough old thing and I'm able to appreciate these same three plants each springtime before broad-leaved sedges and coarse grasses swallow them up for another year.

Over the brook, though the gate and into an open field, gangs of St Mark's flies patrol the air. These shiny-black insects emerge on cue each year at around the same time as the festival of the feast of St Mark (April 25th), give or take a cold snap, and can then be seen for a few weeks as hanging swarms, moving languidly up and down, dangling their distinctively long hind legs, patrolling the space just above head height. The males of the species have the enviable evolutionary ability to look in two directions at the same time, their eyes divided into upper and lower parts with separate connections to the brain. It is perhaps fortunate that we do not possess the same ability, or else we might spend all our time staring into our phones whilst going about our daily lives (although give it a few hundred years...).

The fly, being a fly, has no use for such distracting technology, and employs its upper eye-part to look out for females, whilst the lower section monitors its position relative to the ground. Flies tend to hold a very different place in our hearts than, say, colourful bumbling bees, but they are just as important when it comes to the pollination of our flowers and crops. It is unfortunate that while many species of fly perform such beneficial functions, in the minds of many they are still much maligned, stuck with the tag of being unhygienic and unwelcome, inextricably linked to turds and muck and rotting carcasses, rather than to our favourite fruits, vegetables and nuts, the unsung heroes helping to provide our five-a-day.

The Cuckoo (Part II)

The form, patterning and flight of a cuckoo bears a remarkable resemblance to another bird to be feared by passerines, the sparrowhawk. This cunning visual deception helps in the female cuckoo's first objective following mating, as songbirds tend to hide from hawks passing overhead, and so are more likely to leave their nest exposed for a brief moment when spotting the silhouette of a potential predator.

The cuckoo, famously, does not bother to build its own home but rather lays a single egg in the occupied nest of another bird. In other words, it is a brood parasite. Around here cuckoos can be heard calling in woodland, where the most common host is the dunnock, and in water meadows and the fringes of waterways, where the reed warbler lives. The means by which a cuckoo manages to lay its egg in another's nest, and then deceive the host into both accepting the egg and rearing a substantially larger chick that the host produces, is truly remarkable and extremely underhand.

In less than the time it takes to read this sentence, the female cuckoo is able to land in a vacated nest, lay an egg, and depart. Speed of laying is essential because if the host spots the cuckoo, it is much more likely to reject the egg. The act of a cuckoo laying her egg is rarely observed, but the call of the female immediately after egg laying is occasionally heard. I've heard the noise once – a loud, macabre, unearthly 'chuckling' sound – and it stopped me in my tracks. Logically, it would seem to make no sense that such a secretive bird would emit such an obvious call, and it is only very recently that behavioural ecologists have come to understand why the female appears to draw attention to her act of villainy. Whilst the 'cuck-oo' call of the male has no effect whatsoever on the vigilance of the host bird in its nest, the 'chuckle' of the female has the same influence as the call of a predatory hawk in distracting the host's attention. So not only does the cuckoo resemble a hawk in shape and flight, it is also capable of mimicking the sound of a sparrowhawk to enhance the chances of the host being momentarily diverted from the task of guarding her nest and precious eggs.

4th May

South-easterly winds gusting to sixty miles per hour haul mountainous cloud formations towering a mile or more into the village skies. Layers of pewter cloud skid under white cumulus ranges, unloading intense showers before speeding away to reveal first blue holes and then clear skies for the swallows and skylarks to fill, making the most of the warmth before a new formation blows in and the next wave hits. Light is chased along roads, pavements, tracks and fields, scanning the landscape, its intensity flickering, constantly changing. The sound of the rain is different from a few weeks ago, filtered by leaves rather than allowed to pass unopposed through bare branches, drops then ricocheting off the surfaces of herbs freshly unfurled, on wood dock, dog's mercury and burdock, before colliding with the hard earth. Each drenching sounds like a rush of applause. The rain leaves a wet sheen covering stones and grasses, turning cracked tracks mocha brown, bursts of brilliant warm sunlight releasing the intoxicating aroma of damp earth drying.

6th May

Whilst oak canopies are filling out with translucent apple-green leaves, the branches of most of the ash trees are still bare, good news if you plan your summer holidays around the confident maxim that states 'oak before ash you're in for a splash, ash before oak you're in for a soak'. In reality, the leafing of the two species almost exclusively depends upon spring temperatures and has precisely nothing to do with rainfall in summer, but still, I'll take the prediction for this year. For two mature ash trees in the pasture behind our house, however, the race to leaf first is over. They lack not only leaves and flowers, but black buds too. Dark-brown lesions have developed at the point where branches meet the trunk. Their brittle limbs snap rather than bend in the wind. Stiff crowns stripped of bark surrender to the sky. These trees, after over two centuries rooted in this field, have been infected by a fungus (*Hymenoscyphus fraxineus*) that has the potential to be as devastating to our native ash as another fungus (*Ophiostoma novo-ulmi* [8]) has been to our once statuesque elms.

Commonly known as ash dieback disease, it is caused by spores produced by the fungus from tiny white fruiting bodies that develop in fallen leaf litter. These microscopic spores are released into the atmosphere and can travel many tens of miles before they land, sticking to and then penetrating ash leaves. The fungus then grows inside the tree, eventually blocking water transport systems, but it is not a quick death, and the trees do resist, still flickering with life, partially dressed in summer, though many succumb to multiple infections over a few years, ultimately resulting in their demise. The trees in the pasture now stand almost lifeless, save for a giant bracket fungus at the base of one, and a woodpecker nest within a neat hole two thirds of the way up the trunk of the other.

The ash is by far the most common mature tree in the village, following the loss of the elms. Without them our landscape would again be irrevocably transformed. It is impossible to contemplate, but then the same was probably true fifty years ago when the elms started to die. Perhaps their loss will be so gradual and piecemeal that

[8] AKA Dutch Elm disease

we will forget how common they once were, an integral part of hedgerows and lanes and woodland, fading from the landscape and from memory with each successive generation. Yet there is a glimmer of hope. Results of recent research suggest that perhaps as many as half of all ash trees are tolerant to the dieback disease. As a prolific producer of seed, this might mean that resistant ash populations could eventually recover in the decades to follow. But still, for many mature trees, death comes on swift winds.

8th May

An impressive thunderstorm briefly envelops the village, causing the dog to tremble under my desk as rain batters against windows and roof tiles. It soon passes, the dog recovers his equilibrium and I start off to the woodland, impatient to see the progress of the spring flora. A pungent, sweet, somewhat stomach-churning smell of acid-yellow oilseed rape fills the air, along with songbirds and mewing buzzards, all drying out under a warming sun. The surface of the green lane is slippery underfoot, the recent downpour turning the upper couple of centimetres to mud above a solid base. Field ditches full with watercress and water figwort are already taking in rainwaters from neighbouring arable fields. Bright-blue speedwells, lemon-yellow cowslips and turquoise forget-me-nots flourish along their sloping banks, emphasising the contrast with monocultures either side.

By the time I reach the entrance to an ancient part of the wood, the scent of hawthorn in full bloom has overpowered distant rape crops. The hawthorn flowers have a complicated, musky perfume thick with almonds but with jarringly fishy undertones. The smell is divine to some, verging on repulsive to others. My receptors fall on the 'divine' side of the debate. It draws me in through a gap in the hedge, into dappled sunlight and a patchwork of blue, white and green layering the ground beneath gnarled multi-stemmed field maples, spreading hazel coppice and sturdy oaks, some wrapped in ivy with stems as thick as my leg. Black ash buds have begun to split open, releasing pinnate leaves held to attention on long green stalks. I've chosen a good time to visit, as the recent thunderstorm, and especially the heavy rain, has helped to cleanse the air of dust, aerosols and other particulates and has, through gravity, released chemical compounds bound up in the earth and vegetation, heightening woodland scents. Stooping to kneel, I bury my nose into a patch of violet bells and creamy anthers, getting as close as the bumblebees that are busy mining for nectar nearby. Their heads must be buzzing with the intoxicating smell of thousands of bluebell flowers by the end of each day.

It is an afternoon of constantly changing light. Clouds shift the tones of the woodland floor. The scent of drifts of wild garlic blend with hawthorn and bluebells to activate memories of a childhood spent living by a woodland that stretched from the steep road below our house down to open grassland where games were played and knees were split, on to a pebble-strewn beach to search for fragments of coloured glass pummelled and smoothed by the waves, to rockpools with hermit crabs and bright-green snakelocks anemones.

I weave my way along narrow desire lines created by roaming deer and badger, past wide mossy stumps stubbornly rooted to their place, under arches of crab apple crowded with spoon-shaped petals. Hawthorn buds deep within the wood have yet to burst open, and the scent of garlic takes over. Although this woodland is not as floristically diverse as some in nearby parishes, the lack of rarities is more than compensated for by an abundance of colour and fragrance. I pause to lean against the trunk of an oak and hidden species begin to appear: broad, arrow-shaped leaves of cuckoo pint, small mauve flowers of ground ivy, the happy faces of dog violets, unfurling shuttlecock fronds of male and scaly male ferns.

The light fades again, a light rain falls, the garlic leaves crackle. A large gap in the canopy reveals rumbling slate-grey storm clouds, silencing birdsong. My inner ears become sore, detecting a sudden change in air pressure, and it strikes me momentarily that walking in a wood at this precise moment is probably not the best place to be. But the storm soon passes and blue skies return.

I wander for a time through a section of spruce and pine plantation, either lost or exploring depending on your point of view. Some of the conifers are marked at chest height with bright splodges of red paint, their time almost up. I cross back into broadleaves and the wind picks up, rustling the canopies above, a sound that has been absent for so long. Wide grassy rides dressed in shadow and light lead me to a familiar hard-standing track that bisects the wood and marks the western limits of the village boundary. This is the place where purple emperor butterflies will be sought out in a month or so, the rides full of enthusiasts who travel here in the hope of catching a glimpse of this majestic insect. Just now, though, I have the place to myself as I stroll along, nestled within a woodland that has, once more, stirred into spring.

11th May

Swifts have made a welcome return to the skies, stiff boomerang-winged thunderbolts set loose on the winds, cutting through clouds of insects and the verdant smell of lush vegetation. Whilst the swifts patrol above, agile swallows and house martins glide over the flat-calm waters of the gravel pits, their reflections rising to meet them as they stoop to skim the surface, perfect mirror images then falling away as they loop and turn to snaffle their breakfast. The birds come to rest every now and again in a thin patch of browned reed. Some land for a few seconds on spent flower heads, bending plumes to their weight. Others clasp hollow rigid stems, a more secure landing station. Reed and sedge warblers sing out their complex notes from the sidelines as the swallows and martins lift off to repeat their mesmeric swooping twisting patterns, a scene of serenity only a few months ago played out by these same birds amongst baobabs, proteas, elephants and springbok in the heat of an African summer.

15th May

The farmer is busy in his wheat fields, chugging back and forth, a steady stream of small white fertiliser pellets flowing down from a large container fixed to the rear of his tractor, falling onto two large whirring metal discs below, set at a slight angle. They bounce off at speed, a constant fine spray of hail scattered over the soil in a ten-metre arc, its contents then slowly released to feed the growing crop, which will eventually feed us. As the farmer is completing his final run, passing close to the path which leads down to the brook, we wave at each other. Seconds later I feel the sharp sting of a few errant pellets hitting my face. I'll ask him later if the smile he gave me was a knowing one.

The burgeoning wheat crop looks like it has been undersown with poppies, such is their profusion. Thousands of plants provide a dense ground cover of light green leaves, contrasting with the glaucous wheat. If they aren't killed off by herbicide, they will provide a spectacular flowering display in the summer. Admittedly, it's a big 'if'. Yellow compact heads of charlock and black mustard are scattered amongst the poppy leaves, synchronising their flowering time with fields of another brassica, oilseed rape, glowing on the horizon.

The wide unploughed margin at the bottom of the field linking magnificent crack willows with reeds and the river is fast becoming a jungle of cow parsley, three feet high and rising, a curtain of white frothy heads stretching uninterrupted for half a kilometre, successfully fighting for space with nettles, burdock and hogweed. Though these are all ubiquitous species, they will provide an abundance of food for the surrounding wildlife throughout the spring and summer months. The broad margin also ensures that the contents of the fertiliser pellets do not reach the river, which is good news not just for aquatic life but also for the 'wild swimmers' who patrol the waters in brightly coloured headgear, towing luminous floats in their wake.

The Cuckoo (Part III)

The cuckoo produces an egg that, to us, looks remarkably similar to the host egg, but birds see colour differently to humans; we have three colour cones (red, green, blue) but birds have four, being able to also see ultra-violet. When looked at in this way, the match between the cuckoo egg and the host egg is exceptional, miraculous even.

Recent studies have demonstrated that the fussier the host bird, the better the cuckoo is at egg mimicry. But in a battle of wits, as the cuckoo becomes more adept at mimicking the pattern of the host egg, the host becomes more proficient at designing eggs with a more complex 'signature'. The cuckoo does not always win this war, but if their egg is accepted and the cuckoo chick does hatch, it is never rejected by the host mother even though it is obvious, at least to us, that it is plainly not related. And the cuckoo chick isn't in the slightest bit interested in bonding with its new foster siblings.

17th May

At half-past seven in the evening it is lighter than it has been all day, the rain clouds retreating to become immense formations on the horizon. My boots shimmer through the wet grass. Chiffchaffs, robins, blackbirds and song thrushes compete for stretches of hedge and field. Down at the ridge and furrow water meadow that joins with the river, a cuckoo calls over dots of nodding meadow buttercups and the fragile globes of thousands of geometric dandelion clocks, their whiteness exaggerated by verdant grassland and taking on a faint luminosity in the last hour or so of daylight. It is perfectly still, and the air is filled with hawthorn scent and thousands of tiny flies moving erratically within their own tightly defined spaces. A male curlew calls every so often, a bubbling, evocative crescendo that adds so much to the landscape, a sound memorably described by W.H. Hudson[9] as seemingly "uttered by some filmy being, half spirit and half bird".

While the furrows still hold water, the ridges that curve above them are comparatively dry and speckled white with meadow saxifrage, the first floral star of the season. Its clusters of pure white, five-petalled bell-shaped flowers sit on graceful stems glistening due to an abundance of tiny glandular hairs, each dotted with a minute sticky blob. Their kidney-shaped leaves hide tiny pinkish-red bulbils, which later in the season may be trodden on and dispersed in the hooves of cattle, or carried on flood waters to pastures new, where some might go on to form a new rosette of leaves and flower in the years to follow. This is the saxifrage's main means of moving around the countryside; in some respects, the flowers are simply for show. The appearance of the bulbils led to them being used in the distant past by herbalists in an attempt to break up gall and kidney stones – the plant's name literally translates as 'rock-breaker' (*Saxifraga*) 'with grain' (*granulata*). I suppose that desperate times called for desperate measures.

Walking closer to the river's edge I spot two curlews feeding in the soft ground fringing a large pool of rainwater, their slate-brown shapes well camouflaged in comparison to the chunky shelducks in the shallows

---

[9] A naturalist writing in the late 19th and early 20th centuries, and author of *A Shepherd's Life*

of a nearby rain-filled depression, and the half-hidden gangs of black-headed gulls, jackdaws and rooks dotted throughout the meadow. The curlews walk gracefully along the margins of the pool, elegant legs now visible, long curved bills probing the mud. The female is clearly larger when seen next to the male who follows close behind, mirroring its partner's movements. Although it is a pleasure to see these birds, the fact that both are now visible suggests that in all likelihood their nest has failed. It is unlikely that they will try again this year.

Freshly hatched, feebly airborne puffs of invertebrates drift a few metres above the surface of the river, picked off a mouthful at a time by swooping house martins and swallows. By the riverbank a few snails cling to last year's purple loosestrife stems, dangling perilously close to a current given away by the gentle wobble of slender bullrushes marking the boundary of rooted liminal vegetation. In ripples created by skimming insects and hungry fish, the river reflects blue and grey, white, pink and gold. The sun dips into a sliver of open sky sandwiched between long clouds and tall willows. It casts a broad beam that lights up and cuts in two the water meadow, spotlighting geese grazing in distant wheat fields and illuminating black-headed gulls as they whirl away in the direction of the gravel pits, off to spend the night at their communal roost.

23rd May

Lambs and ewes are being moved out of exhausted fields, dogs and whistles, shouts and claps herding them down the road, past houses and waiting traffic, into ungrazed fields flush with the growth brought on by a warm sun and sharp showers. The lambs have filled out, legs now sturdy and supporting an ever-increasing bulk.

I walk past the wary sheep, carefully step over the barbed fence and head down to the brook through waist-high cow parsley, disturbing freshly emerged banded demoiselles and minding out for burrow entrances half hidden in the thick grass. Beneath the surface of the water, tadpoles are resting on silt-covered rocks. They are harder to catch than I remember, their wiggling tails propelling them to safety, and it takes a few scoops before I have a couple in my cupped palms. No sign of legs yet, but their rounded bodies have a dusting of gold leaf that shimmers in the dappled light. I release them back into the murky water and pick my way back along exposed rocks and patches of fool's watercress, feeling ten years old again. Climbing back over the fence and out of the shelter of the brook, it slowly dawns on me that the sheep are lying down, their bellies resting on dry grass. The wind has picked up, and the light has dulled. I look over my shoulder to see a sweeping grey curtain heading my way.

Striding briskly across the field and jumping over a wooden fence, I head towards a line of alders and crouch behind their knotted boles. Resting against a thick trunk I gaze out at the river as it begins to boil, feeling smug about managing to keep relatively dry in the midst of such a downpour. A remarkably tranquil scene presents itself, with the life surrounding me silent and still, waiting for the rain to pass. After a while the river's surface becomes smooth once more, a curlew's fluttering call gives the all clear, and it is only then that I notice white flowers within the tall sedge thinly spread around me. I look more closely at the leaves by my wet boots, and realise that the weather has pushed me into a large population of marsh valerian, a vanishingly rare plant around here, with just one other site nearby, a protected nature reserve. Most aren't flowering, not surprising really as they are growing under quite deep shade, when what they really crave is more open and light conditions. The leaves themselves look fairly unremarkable, like small dull docks, but the pink-tinged, slightly triangular white heads of the few that are in flower are remarkably elegant, held on long, upright, ridged stems. They must have been here for some considerable time given the size of the population, fed by the springs that upwell through limestone bedrock to meet the surface of the pasture further up the slope.

The constant trickling of lime-rich water to the spot where the valerian grows creates the base-rich conditions it and a few other plants nearby require, such as stunted forms of greater tussock sedge which I also missed in my haste as I leapt from the rain shower. A jumble of other species marks out a prolonged absence of grazing but also indicates imperceptible changes to topography, hydrology and water chemistry. Some are associated with dry woodland, such as the dog's mercury, wild garlic and enchanter's nightshade growing on raised ground created by the alder roots and the shade that its canopy casts, while the pond sedge and especially patches of yellow iris, not quite in flower, suggest deeper saturated soils for roots that can withstand prolonged periods of anoxia caused by regular flooding from the river. At the micro-scale there are mosses associated with acidic substrates adorning the base on an alder stump where rainwater collects, providing a stark contrast to their lime-loving neighbours.

I had often wondered what would in the past have grown in the grassy seepages the sheep now graze, in the years before the field was resown with a prescribed list of grasses. It would seem feasible that, perhaps more than a century ago, parts of this field might have resembled the protected ancient patch of species-rich fen that still survives by the gravel pits. It is pleasing to find such a vivid memory persisting in the shadows, even if it has been pushed to the margins.

31st May

The arable fields that climb the steep gradient to meet woodland have recently been sown with barley. As I make my way up the slope, evenly spaced drilled rows of young fresh leaves stretch into the distance. The young crop appears more densely coloured-in on the curves and dips, then vanishes on the flat, an illusion brought about by an undulating topography and my shifting position in the landscape.

It is noticeably cooler when inside the wood, blue skies now framed by thick branches with full canopies. Many of the bluebells hold green pods instead of nodding lilac and cobalt blooms. Nettles have begun to dominate the ground flora as wild garlic leaves wilt to yellows and browns. Wearing shorts was probably not the wisest choice.

I look up to see that an ash tree directly above my head has recently snapped about ten feet from its base, but has not been completely severed from its body. It is instead resting at a jaunty angle of about 45°, propped against the crown of a nearby oak. It appears safe enough, at least until the next gale. Along its trunk is a series of perfectly circular holes. I was drawn to this area by the rapid, high-pitched noise of hungry chicks, hard to place at first but which appears to be coming from one of the entrances high above. The frequency and volume intensify as a different call, a sharp loud 'kiik', comes from nearby and a male great-spotted woodpecker comes into view, his beautiful pied plumage set off by a brilliant-red rump and a scarlet patch that covers the back of his head. He hops his way up and around the trunk of a large oak, picking food from crevices, occasionally battering the bark to release what I assume are hidden grubs. The chicks, seemingly masters of circular breathing, maintain their relentless, piercing plea.

Moving a short distance away, I rest at the base of an ash trunk upholstered with dry, velvet-soft moss and wait for the parent bird to reveal which of the many holes hides the nest. The first section of my seat is curved like a hammock for the first three metres or so, hovering just above the ground before bolting twelve metres straight up towards the light. The vertical part of the trunk rocks gently in the breeze. Many of the trees in this part of the wood have similar bends and cambers, harking back to a time when they emerged from the shadows of their elders, searching for the light. It is not long before the woodpecker swoops to the base of the uppermost hole and pokes his head inside. Hungry begging calls become louder for a few seconds as food is dished out, then the adult departs to find another meal, the sound of endlessly hungry chicks ringing in his ears.

Scanning the length of the trunk it is clear that one of the lower holes made by woodpeckers over the years is also full of life. Just above the point where the shaft has snapped, a constant stream of honeybees enter and exit their secret nest. Honeybees setting up home so close to a woodpecker nest could be viewed as a bold decision, as these birds have been known to eat bees in harsh winters, although in a woodland humming with life it is unlikely that they will be disturbed for now.

Inside the tree they will be busy constructing honeycomb, forager bees returning to the hive with nectar which they pass on to receiver bees, who in turn process the honey and store it in waxy cells, or if the comb is well stocked, share the payload with other bees nearby. The comb will provide a vital food source in the winter months when there are fewer flowers to harvest. It is a highly efficient system perfected over millions of years. Long before humans 'domesticated' bees so that we could take advantage of their delicious produce, wild nests such as the one I'm now watching were eagerly sought out. There is evidence for the practice of 'bee hunting' in ancient cave paintings found in Valencia which depict a woman climbing a vine and putting her hand inside a swarming nest. As someone who has a sweet tooth, I wonder if I would have done the same, or more likely waited a safe distance away for the honey to come to me.

I watch the bees for a while, contemplating how busy they are and how relaxed I am. After a while I force myself to vacate my very comfortable perch and move further into the wood. It strikes me just how many mature field maples, one of my favourite trees, there are in this small area. Almost all of them seem to have been coppiced in the distant past; that is to say their branches were cut and left to grow for about five years, before being cut back again, with the cycle then repeated. Most of the crop was probably used for either charcoal or firewood. But for a good hundred years the maples have been left alone, with the result that many now boast multiple wizened stems. They are wonderfully characterful, with each sporting different patterns of knobbly epicormic growths that themselves sprout tiny branches with leaves that tightly clothe the trunk. As I'm examining one particularly gnarly specimen, I catch sight in my peripheral vision of background movement deeper within the wood. With binoculars I see first one and then multiple fallow deer, a mass of heads and speckled bodies gathered together in a sunny gap. For a few minutes I have marvellous views as they feed along an open ride, pointed ears swivelling like radar dishes, constantly alert to the dangers around them.

Deer numbers have increased substantially over the years due to a variety of reasons, not least the unintentional introduction into the wild of the muntjac, now a near-ubiquitous sight in southern England. Although if you want to get really picky, the fallow isn't native either, brought across by the Normans a thousand years ago. While a wild deer is a truly beautiful sight, as an ecologist I know that 'too many' is very much not a 'good thing' for the carpets of bluebells, regenerating trees, and the abundance of life that depends on the retention of a scrubby understorey. Culling deer is a difficult message to sell, and the 'Bambi factor' tends to dominate the argument. It is quite reasonable to question what right one species (us) has to kill another (them) in order to restore what we perceive to be the correct balance, especially as humans have been responsible for both their presence and the destruction of so much ancient woodland, continuing to put profit and ease of travel before the natural world. But in the absence of a few lynxes or the odd wolf, and with the ongoing suicidal clearance of pristine rainforest for western meat consumption, perhaps the carnivores amongst us might look to locally sourced venison as an ecologically sustainable solution, instead of cheap beef flown in from the other side of the world.

Following a route created by the deer, through the thick fug of hawthorn blossom, past freshly unfurled fronds and filled badger latrines, I step over fallen branches resting into the soil, now more moss and rot than solid wood, and after numerous stings on idiotically bare legs, emerge from the wood into bright sunlight and the highest point of the parish. A mammoth grey carbuncle of a warehouse on the horizon does its best to blend in, but it is trying too hard. Red kites fly in the distance at eye level, livestock shrink to dots in pastures and a few garish fields of oilseed rape glow, incongruous amidst the subtle colours of an English spring. Near the gateway to the top pasture a bloated sheep lies on its back, legs stiff, long dead, ready to pop. Its companions graze nearby, seemingly oblivious. I wander downhill, cutting a narrow channel through dense clouds of shoulder-high cow parsley, blue shorts and t-shirt soon coated with a fine dusting of pollen. I pass magnificent boundary oaks that have seen over three hundred springs, have heard the calls of chiffchaff, cuckoos, exploding wrens and melodic willow warblers that provide the soundtrack to my descent.

A vibrant wash of colour takes me completely by surprise as I emerge to break the cover of the narrow track. I have often walked across these lower fields, floristically dulled as a consequence of past herbicide use, and they have always been closely cropped by sheep or cattle, displaying only a bright green uniformity that kept my eyes fixed firmly on the horizon. I had long ago given up on them. But livestock have clearly not yet been here this year, and perennial herbs previously suppressed by hungry mouths over springs past have taken this opportunity to remind me of their resilience and common beauty. I stroll leisurely amongst bulbous and meadow buttercups that light up the way, the latter rising on delicate stems above red clover and daisies. Waves of yellow, pink, crimson, red and white flow in complex patterns amongst grasses that can finally display their individuality – bromes, fescues, foxtail, sweet vernal. The fields have transformed into an aesthetically uplifting sight, and each step disturbs the buzz of bees, beetles, hoverflies, moths, butterflies and numerous other mini-beasts. Messed about with and degraded compared to past glories these fields may be, but tell that to the wildlife that still call this place their home.

As I reach the last field before the lane I'm met by a couple of ramblers, the first people I have seen all afternoon. Like me, they have binoculars draped around their necks, and we fall into the inevitable 'seen much?' chat, as opposed to the equally ubiquitous 'nice/awful weather' conversation. They tell me of rarities sighted, of

garden warblers and a hobby's nest, but seem reluctant
to let me know the precise location of the nest. To be
fair to them, I probably do look a bit dishevelled and
untrustworthy. I tell them of the woodpecker, the bees
and the deer. They seem deeply unimpressed, and there
are a few seconds of awkward silence before they walk
briskly on their way.

4th June

The grass is now sufficiently lush for cows and their calves
to be turned out into the top field behind our house. It
is lovely watching the youngsters let loose, their hooves
up to this point knowing only hard concrete floors.
Their arrival is also good news for flies, although in this
regard the cows' burden is slightly eased by a small flock
of starlings that rise up from hidden positions in the
long grass, making their way along backs and rumps
and heads to pick off at least a few of the unwelcome
visitors. It is not quite like the Serengeti with cattle
egrets and wildebeests, but the principle is much the
same. The calves seem a bit more relaxed than last year's
lot, when I watched one so deliriously happy at finding
its feet on soft grassland for the first time that it ran
and kicked and danced across the field to the boundary

edge, its momentum carrying it on to the top of the barbed wire fence where it performed a spectacular cartwheel, landing hooves first into the adjoining field of wheat.

The cows spend a good part of their day resting and digesting, often gathering near to two ash trees, one rising high above them, its leaves only recently released from buds, the other a fallen top lying next to its shattered stump, a casualty of a violent summer storm a few years ago. It has been left where it fell, partly because its removal is not a high priority for a busy farmer, but also because the trunk and prostrate branches make perfect scratching posts for the cows to rub up against. It also distracts the cows from the potential relief of concrete posts that hold up our wire fence, the only barrier between a bucolic scene and a wrecked garden.

They don't yet have access to any of the lower fields, and I'm soon over a few gates and by the river, followed all the way by the scent of hawthorn flowers amplified on a warm and sunny afternoon, the essence of late spring. A long flood meadow is thick with meadow buttercups doing a fine job at mimicking an impressionist's brushstrokes. The field hasn't been sprayed with herbicide for many decades and has gradually become flower rich, although not nearly as diverse as its exclusively unsprayed neighbour. But it makes a perfect spot for nesting waders, and especially the lapwing, whose chicks will have fledged by the time the cattle make their way down here. It is also good hiding and hunting ground for hares and, with an abundance of voles, barn owls are regular visitors too. In amongst the buttercups, marsh ragwort is dotted about, a far more elegant plant to my eye than its blacklisted cousin. I follow the river, walking against its flow, through shifting swarms of beige insects until I reach the stone bridge and the road that leads back to the village. A song thrush high in an oak tree sings me home.

9th June

The ash trees have, at last, filled the final few gaps in what is now a lush landscape brim-full with song, scent, structure, colour and movement. And pollen, lots of pollen, a disproportionate amount of which seems to be attracted to my eyes as a nagging itch dares me to do something about it. The urge to react can be overwhelming, and whilst taking the bait can for the first second or two provide blessed relief, I know well that even the slightest rub will simply intensify the desire to rub, quickly resulting in a vicious circle of tear-filled, swollen red eyes, and more rubbing. Time to find the antihistamines.

Spring rains and a prolonged spell of warm weather have resulted in meadows transformed into deep seas, their background haze of chlorophyll enhancing the brilliance of the more obvious blooms such as the broad white domes of hogweed, long slender strips of ox-eye daisy and the last throes of cow parsley. Whilst these provide welcome colour to the landscape, the real gems lie within, hidden in plain sight.

I walk to a random spot in the ancient ridge and furrow water meadow and crouch down to survey the scene, elbows resting on knees that hover above the damp soil. Parting the dirty-orange flowering heads of marsh foxtail reveals a sprawling patch of tufted forget-me-not, each azure flower only a few millimetres across and branded with a central yellow ring. As I move a few paces on, scattering insects into the air, a second location divulges a slightly different mix. The grasses are much the same, but with a few strands of spike-rush that have subtle differences to the usual type. This is slender spike-rush, for which there is only one site in the county – this field. It grows amongst a liberal scattering of ragged robin, its flowers resembling a nodding swathe of intricate papercutting, all candy-striped calyces and delicate deeply incised pink petals.

Batting away a stubborn horsefly, I move on to a third spot in one of the furrows nearby. It holds a few plants of amphibious bistort, elegant slender tufted sedge and a smattering of floating sweet-grass, the latter's pale flowering stems curving over its companions, a sure sign that this area was under water for much of the autumn and winter. A fourth place in a seemingly similar furrow is more diverse, with the spiky fruiting heads of marsh marigold alongside tufted forget-me-not, ragged robin and a delicate carpet of marsh bedstraw growing with an abundance of tubular water-dropwort. This last plant is a bit of a speciality around here, found in cattle-grazed grasslands along the river corridor. Its flowers are nothing to write home about. They are small, white and clumped together at the top of a pale-green hollow stem. But what a stem, especially when backlit to reveal delicate lateral striations.

You could fill a book (and people have) about the plants of such water meadows. I have recorded upwards of 150 plant species in this small patch of ancient turf.

They give away subtle differences in soils, hydrology and topography. They mark the weaving mycelium of fungal associates and the grazing patterns of livestock. They tell tales of hidden gravel under a sward where once, long ago, a river flowed. These plants speak of a complexity gradually accreted over centuries, culminating in natural patterns impossible for us to replicate. This meadow is a survivor partly by chance, partly by location. It has depended, and continues to depend, on the actions of generations of stockmen and farmers. Such places are unique to the environment they sit within. They comprise a mindboggling diversity of life, fix carbon, support livelihoods, give pleasure and hope. And in many areas, they have been insidiously airbrushed from our landscape by the flick of a switch or the turn of a blade, erasing what was waiting to be discovered, what will only be missed by those who care to look.

The Cuckoo (Part IV)

Within days of hatching, the blind newborn chick wastes no time in cleansing the nest, dispatching all the eggs laid by the host bird, one by one, using a hollow in its broad back and the leverage of long legs to push the eggs over the side. If the host's eggs have already hatched then the cuckoo will eject the other much smaller chicks in the same manner, to their certain death. Other parasitic cuckoo species that live in different parts of the world use different methods. The New World cuckoos, for example, have a small hook at the end of their beak which they use to slash the host chicks to death.

Once the competition is ruthlessly dispatched, the cuckoo is the sole recipient of food brought by the oblivious surrogate parents. But why do they feed a chick that is so demonstrably unlike them, and will after two weeks be seven times their size and considerably larger than the nest? And how does the chick trick its foster parents into bringing it enough food? It is again all down to mimicry. Reed warblers are tuned in to listen to the begging call of their chicks, of which there are usually four. They also pay close attention to the size of a chick's gape. The cuckoo chick has a fairly large gape relative to one reed warbler chick, but it is not nearly as large as four chicks, and so the cuckoo has yet another trick up its sleeve – vocal mimicry. The cuckoo is capable of producing a rapid begging call which sounds to the adult providing food like a whole brood of hungry chicks. And as the cuckoo gets older it is able to increase the frequency of the begging call and sustain its supersized diet by sounding like the equivalent of two broods of reed warbler chicks. This deception eventually leads to a full belly, fledging and migration, leaving its worn-out cuckolded host with an empty nest and nothing to show for its prodigious efforts, save for an oversized bird that may one day return to ransack another warbler brood.

12th June

One of the more glamorous insects of the parish is on the wing. Alongside numerous small damselflies, roaming matchsticks with abdomens of brilliant blues, greens, and reds interrupted by black segments, the banded demoiselle stands out. For a start it is much larger than the others, with a wingspan of about 6cm. They flutter gracefully over vegetation close to the river like tightly wound clockwork toys released into the wild, broad paddle-shaped wings moving independently to enable high levels of mobility, helping them to compete for territory, catch food and avoid becoming food.

The males have a metallic-blue body, often with flashes of green apparent on the thorax and abdomen as it glints in the sun, and intricately veined translucent wings that look as if they have been pinched between a sooty thumb and forefinger, leaving a broad dusky blue-black residue which flashes in flight. The females are just as magnificent, painted a racing green, but with wings that lack the obvious dusky wing spot, their rounded tips marked instead by a tiny white dot. When at rest they clasp their wings behind them to rest alongside or just above their abdomen. If it wasn't obvious that they weren't dragonflies, this is the clincher, as the latter holds its wings in a horizontally fixed, washboard pose. Whilst I realise that beauty is in the eye of the beholder, it's hard not to be uplifted by the sight of such striking creatures skipping across a flower-rich sward, or skimming the margins of a slow-flowing river.

Dragonflies are a different proposition altogether, finely tuned hunting machines shrunken in size from their peak primordial days but still just as deadly, all whirl and pace and stealth. As I walk along the river's edge to admire the damselflies I almost step on a scarce chaser, motionless and clasping a blade of grass low down in the sward. Once vanishingly rare outside of East Anglia, they have become a regular sight around here in late spring. The dragonfly, seemingly not at all bothered by my presence, is a male. It has matching powder-blue eyes and abdomen, a dark hairy thorax and four tiny black segments on the outer tips of translucent, stained-glass wings. It's a chunky-looking thing oozing power and menace, and although he holds absolutely no threat to me, I give him a wide, respectful berth in the same way you would for any prehistoric creature that has evolved into a perfect killing machine, and wish him luck on his hunt for horseflies.

As the sun begins to set, mayflies appear, seemingly jumping for joy at their one shot at terrestrial life. Cloud columns yo-yo above the vegetation, clear wings beating to lift them vertically a metre or so above the grass, at which point they glide back down to the spot where they started, to begin the loop all over again. Watching mayflies is to be hypnotised, up and down, long hair-like 'tails' streaming out behind them on the ascent, bending upwards on the descent, dancing to the soundtrack of birdsong. All the mayflies in front of me are male, displaying their flying prowess for females who watch their performance from the sidelines. Once a choice is made, a female will fly in to pick her mate, who will fertilise her eggs and then fall to the water with wings outstretched, motionless and near death, easy prey for hungry fish. After the female lays her eggs into the water she will follow her partner into oblivion, their life cycle completed.

The mayfly, like the dragonfly, is an ancient insect, and there are over fifty species in Britain. They belong to the order Ephemeroptera, meaning 'short-lived', which accurately summarises their brief life in flight but not their time underwater, where they may spend up to two years as a larva, or 'nymph'. I'm not sure which species I am watching – a fly fisherman might know – but it seems to be one of the larger ones, with evenly placed dark triangular markings running down its abdomen. I count a dozen or so males but as the sun begins to meet the horizon and the angle of light becomes shallower, hundreds, maybe thousands become visible, backlit in a golden haze, making the most of their finite time, present in the same space where their ancestors danced, long before we put a name to them.

14th June

A thirty-minute bike ride from my front door takes me up the hill into the woods, along rutted, juddery tracks, past recent forestry ride clearance work that currently looks cataclysmic but will in time soften to benefit wildlife that craves such open edge conditions. I swerve to avoid a family of stoats that bolt across the track, nose to tail, and pedal up to reach the north-western limits of the parish boundary.

Beyond an open five-bar metal gate is one of the best lowland hay meadows in the county. A narrow hardstanding track divides the relatively flat top meadow in two, winding its way to an old farmhouse that is half hidden behind mature trees and shrubs. The house is now used as a retreat for visiting artists. If they can't gain inspiration here, they may as well find something else to be getting on with. The bottom meadow, just on from the sharp dogleg that leads to the farmhouse, is ridge and furrow and follows gently rolling topography. It is also split in two, this time by the route of a brook, currently dry and invisible for much of the year under a thick sward. The brook runs from east to west, collecting for a time in a large depression where two enormous white willows grow, their trunks over five metres in diameter, each supporting huge fissured branches, one resembling a giant rhinoceros's head complete with an oversized horn that curves down to touch the turf. This willow has a large hollow at the junction between the trunk and one of the thick branches, home to a family of long-eared owls. The meadow's southern and eastern boundaries abut ancient woodland. To the west are impenetrable hedgerows screening rolling arable fields. A deep strip of willow, thorns, roses, brambles, ash and oak leads to an enormous barley field that blankets the northern boundary, leading to more old woodland that softens the horizon.

Just over a century ago the wood behind me, within the parish, not only comprised standard trees and coppice but also a patchwork of pastures and hay meadows which, I like to imagine, were as rich as the one I'm standing in. Such vanished fields were long ago planted with conifers, but somehow the two meadows here survived, most likely because the farmer still required them for hay production and grazing land. In fact, they have done rather more than survive. They have flourished, avoiding the plague of herbicide that swept through the countryside in the mid 20th century. It is not just that these fields hold rare species, although they do; green-winged orchids are thickly scattered on the higher ridges in late May, and sulphur clover is now coming into flower on the edges of dips and furrows. The feature that really marks this place out as special is the sheer abundance of each species of plant, rare and common alike. Across both meadows the ratio of herb to grass is about 80:20. Everywhere I step there is a wealth of colour and scent. Every available gap is filled, each footstep cushioned. The sheer profusion of herbs, and in particular the abundance of yellow rattle, combined with low soil fertility, means that even now when growth is almost at its peak, most of the turf does not rise above my shins.

In a good year, common spotted orchids bloom in their hundreds of thousands, transforming the meadows with endless spikes of pale-lilac flowerheads, each of their millions of petals scribbled with a unique signature of thin, dark-purple lines and dots. The tiny, deep blue-magenta flowers of common milkwort pop amongst bands of bird's-foot trefoil, fairy flax, yellow rattle, pignut, red clover, hawkbits, pepper saxifrage, lady's bedstraw, knapweeds and the fruiting heads of cowslip. Swathes of salad burnet dominate tens of square metres, globular flower heads rising en masse, their leaves releasing a strong cucumber aroma when crushed underfoot. Ribbons of metallic-pink betony cover the ground sloping down to the northern margin. Tens of thousands of adder's tongue ferns jostle for space with pyramidal orchids, hoary ragwort, meadow buttercups, hoary plantain and slender ox-eye daisies, the latter much neater and more elegant than the larger European cultivars that have become a near-ubiquitous sight on sown roadside verges. Plumes of meadowsweet envelop the damper hollows. And then there are the grasses, all indicative of ancient land. Upright brome, downy meadow grass and meadow fescue generously distributed, their flower heads shimmering above quaking grass, red fescue, meadow barley, sweet vernal grass, heath grass and crested hair-grass. All these species, and many more, sharing mycorrhizal connections, fighting for light and space and nutrients, kept in check by blades and machines that cut and bale once a year.

The aroma of this place is subtle, complex and noticeably distinct from the surrounding land – infinitely sweeter, richer, warmer.

On most visits I'll spot a brown hare, or at the very least see its 'form', a depression moulded to its shape where it rests in flattened grasses. The hares have a regular escape route that leads into the woodland edge next to massive wild pear trees, and it intersects in the grassland with dozens of desire lines created by fallow deer who have spent time here recently, judging by the large patches of squashed turf. Although I rarely see much birdlife out in the meadow, save for buzzards and kites, their songs are everywhere, emanating from dense hedgerows and scrubland, farmland fringes and the wood beyond; today I can hear and recognise cuckoos, yellowhammers, corn buntings, wrens, blackbirds, blackcaps, great, blue and long-tailed tits, pheasants, chiffchaffs, starlings.

As for the insect life associated with the meadows, although it is beyond my ability to name even a small fraction of what is here, today I have observed the hunting skills of emperor and scarce chaser dragonflies, disturbed delicate blue-tailed and white-legged damselflies, studied impressive wasp beetles basking on wide leaves in the scrubby margins. Common blue, peacock, meadow brown, comma and speckled wood butterflies, along with chimney sweeper moths, drift and dart, flutter and bask with painted ladies, recently arrived after completing their incredible migratory journey. Metallic-green thick-legged flower beetles, the males with bodybuilder thighs, seem to be everywhere, their iridescence shining against the purple and yellow flowers they feed upon. Metamorphosis is underway within hundreds of creamy, translucent cocoons attached to grass stems, hiding their colourful cargo of five-spot burnet moths. Grasshoppers ping out from hidden places, powerful legs propelling them twenty times their body height. The air hums with foraging bumblebees: white-tailed, buff-tailed, red-tailed mixing with the common carder bee. Each flower attracts some kind of life: tiny shiny black pollen beetles, apple-green crab spiders, a dizzying array of hoverflies and flies, aphids and weevils.

I sit in the shade for a while and watch two gliders silently looping above the meadows, slowly returning from where they were catapulted into the sky, giant wings bent slightly upwards, seeking out thermals revealed by roaming kites. I have spent hundreds of hours in these fields since I first stumbled across them, years ago, when lost in the woods. It is a deeply inspiring, calming place and I always leave reluctantly, feeling privileged to have been present as just another species to share this wonderland for a brief time, not missed when I have gone.

17th June

At half past eight on a perfectly still evening, the sun is still a hand above the horizon, the solstice only a few days away. In hedges that lead out of the village, elders are weighed down with broad white saucers, each containing a mass of tiny flowers with creamy anthers, their appearance replacing spent hawthorn as the dominant, if far more subtle, scent. The elder's umbels are said to be very tasty if dipped in batter and fried, but then in my experience there aren't many foods that suffer from this approach. Feebly anchored blushing petals of rampant wild roses are dislodged with the slightest touch, whites and pinks resting by spindle, hawthorn and the first flush of dogwood blooms. The walls of the disused church and the old rectory opposite glow with brilliant magenta spikes of one of the more successful plants to escape from English gardens, red valerian, covering and overtopping honeyed stone, their roots firmly anchored in cracks and mortarless gaps.

The subjective fashion maxim 'red and green should ne'er be seen' was clearly conceived by folk who had never witnessed an oat field freckled with the backlit diaphanous petals of common and long-headed poppies, the latter a slightly more delicate orange-red. They are joined by thin, dirty-orange flowering heads of black grass, some with blue-tailed damselflies clasped to their stems, setting up home for the night. Both the poppy and the black grass are annual plants but perennial adversaries for arable farmers who crave a 'clean' field. This is especially true of the latter species, which has built up a significant tolerance to the herbicides that kill off most unwanted 'weeds' that naturally infiltrate the crop. The poppies advantage lies in its ability to produce long-lived seeds, some of which may germinate after being buried in the soil for more than fifty years, although the slightest whiff of herbicide will eradicate nascent rosettes. The contrast of colours drift through the crop, down to a broad grassy margin that meets the river's edge.

Emperor dragonflies are still active by the arched stone bridge, hunting a haze of insects swarming in an aureate light. The dragonflies perform quicksilver acrobatics, outrageous turns, flying above the narrow tarmac road that crosses the bridge, then zipping over fast-flowing water surging through wide arches. The setting sun will soon conclude their activity as the temperature falls and the last flickers of warmth leave the air. Batteries drained, the dragonflies will be forced to sit out the gloaming, remaining motionless until cold blood is recharged by the morning sun.

19th June

It rained heavily overnight, knocking out much of the pollen from the air, flattening leggy grasses. Sturdy hogweed plants remain stubbornly upright, their broad umbels humming with bees and flies. Swallows skim effortlessly over a sea of nodding barley, now with long hair-like awns on the turn. The crop, huddled together for support, has survived the storm.

There is something deeply impressive about a planted monoculture, especially one as aesthetically pleasing as a field of barley when transformed by the wind into a rippling, silky mass in constant motion. Add a scattering of poppies, a few towering stems of wild oat and the graceful nodding heads of rye brome, and you have a crop that is both functional and beautiful. The crop may be largely devoid of the biodiversity that is present in a meadow, or even in the rough margins that are spared from the plough, but there is room enough for crops and wildlife, so long as a balance is found. Indeed, it is vital that this balance exists, both for us, for the farmer and for the species which pollinate, devour pests and add life and colour to the landscape. I suppose that my sunny outlook might be very different if this field wasn't within a mixed farm with abundant habitat available for wildlife to flourish. It is no exaggeration to say that the relatively diverse landscape I walk through today is the result of decisions made by three or four people over the past century. They have allowed some hedgerows to grow tall, layered others, reared livestock on flower-rich grasslands free from herbicide, left marginal land to rewild, reduced direct and atmospheric pollution, and put food on our tables. Such a landscape enriches our lives, and such farmers deserve our respect and support. Otherwise, the markets alone will dictate how much diversity remains in another hundred years, and under that scenario I do not like our odds.

Sticking to the path that follows the barley I walk past goat's beard in seed, their large dirty-white geometric globes infusing the grassland edge. The distant call of a cuckoo drifts over from the direction of the river, the bird lost behind towering hedges crowded with elderflower and dogwood, spring gradually turning to summer. I turn to walk downhill to meet a line of tall crack willows, brushing through dense wet grass. By the time I reach the river's edge my jeans have turned a dark blue, soaked by the rain from the night before.

I have come here to explore wet woodland that creeps along the riverside. As I turn away from an open arable landscape and into the dense wood, I spot something very unexpected: almost hidden within the willows is a creature with binoculars, looking out over the expanse of flood meadow. He is just as surprised to see me, but we quickly regain our equilibrium and swap information about hobbies and curlews and lapwings. He confirms what I had feared, that the curlews have failed to rear young this year. Ditto for the lapwings. There is talk of corvids and foxes, and their place in our countryside. I tell him about the couple I met a month or so ago who mentioned nesting hobbies, and he's pleased to hear it, having seen the birds by the edge of the woodland last year.

Leaving him to his flask of coffee and patient observation I carry on into the shadows, alders now dominating the canopy, mosquitoes patrolling the understorey. There are no clear paths, not even deer tracks, just a mass of vegetation and the imprints my squelching footsteps leave behind. I kick through neck-high nettles and clamber over prostrate mossy trunks, flushing craneflies into the air. It is slow going, but I'm in no rush and it's worth it for the feeling of suddenly being in a wild place, far too wet and unruly to farm, hidden between a well-used footpath and the river, its interior guarded by swamp and biting insects. I wade on through nettles, bend back the low branches of an alder that has lost most of its trunk, and it is suddenly lighter, a large clearing surrounded by willow scrub revealing itself.

The clearing has been created by constantly waterlogged soils produced by spring seepages trickling down to find the river, as well as periodic flooding by the river itself. After a few hesitant steps, my feet and ankles disappear into the mud, leaving alarmingly deep impressions, forcing me back to slightly firmer ground, a sucking sound accompanying the extraction of boots. A dense clump of chest-high, sword-shaped iris leaves rise up from the mud just beyond where it seems safe to walk. Their bright-yellow flowers light up a scene dominated by dull greens and browns and dark impenetrable backdrops, tempting me to inch along a fallen, velvet-soft trunk that bridges the impassable terrain, until I'm hovering a foot or so above the swamp and next to the irises. Each flower is freshly opened and in mint condition. There are three large drooping tongue-shaped sepals with veins that turn a chocolate colour as they approach a golden patch near to the base. Above the sepals are three petals, much smaller upright yellow tufts hiding matchstick-slim brown anthers. All the while as I'm studying the flowers, mosquitoes silently land on my hands, neck and face, the only bare skin on offer. A buzzard circles overhead, calling out in alarm, its loud mewing giving away a nest close by, although it's not visible from where I'm precariously perched. The buzzard is joined by the continuous background alarm calls of wrens, a green woodpecker, great tits and blackbirds, all wary of a lumbering stranger invading their space.

I slowly edge my way back along the fallen trunk, pausing every so often to frantically swat away unwanted visitors, and trample a weaving path, often backtracking to avoid deep mud or impassable thickets, on towards the heart of the wet wood. The still air is thick with the smell of disturbed anoxic soils, decomposing matter and metabolising bacteria. Ancient alders, each sporting seven or eight huge stems, erupt from the earth like giant fossilised fingers, blackened and gnarly. I wouldn't be at all surprised to see pterodactyls nesting in their canopies. Just ahead are open areas much larger than the clearing I previously stumbled across, and almost into. Lesser pond sedge, iris, reed sweet-grass and the purple and yellow flowers of bittersweet, a relative of the potato, all sit in extensive belts of glistening mud and rivulets of shallow water that trickles and weaves around leaves and roots. I know that this land is impassable, and yet the pull of new discoveries draws me into the beginnings of a plan to hopscotch across small tufts of grass and rushes to reach what might be firmer ground. But deep down I know that it would be folly to try. This land is out of bounds, safe only for the vast array of insects and micro-organisms that live undisturbed in a small fragment of wilderness. Some places are meant to be left to the imagination.

I move on to higher, drier ground, wade through another nettle patch, trip over the reddened, hollow carcass of what must have been a very large tree in its day, now disintegrating into the consistency of crumbling soil, its lignin broken down by an unseen fungal network adapted to this humid environment and slowly returning its mass to feed the soil, and the nettles.

Carrying on to where I hope to eventually meet a firm path, squelching through mats of creeping bent grass, the ground flora changes suddenly, an indication of marginally higher and drier ground that is filled with dog's mercury and the yellowing leaves of fading wild garlic. Narrow deer tracks appear under elm and ash and oak. I follow one of the lines, break through a thin curtain of bramble and stumble through the veil that connects woodland with open fields. As I do so, I startle my second person of the day, a dog walker who not unreasonably seems quite alarmed at my sudden entrance, his first opinion of me probably not helped by a beard in need of trimming and scruffy clothes saved for fieldwork. I respond to his audible gasp with a squinting, awkward smile, primitive man emerging into the light.

23rd June

On what is, more or less, the longest day of the year, I wake up thinking that it might be a nice idea to go on the longest walk, at least in terms of distance, taking me up to the northernmost boundary of the parish that is marked by a magnificent Elizabethan building. It is about four kilometres measured as a straight line on the map, but more like seven after all of the curves and angles are taken into account. That's a fourteen kilometre round-trip, always assuming I don't get lost or distracted wandering off the designated route, which I will. As it happens, such a walk was never a realistic plan, with too much indoor work to be getting on with, and it is early evening before I'm free to leave the house, far too late to undertake such a lengthy stroll. But the weather is perfect and I haven't been to this area of the parish for a good few months, so I do what any moderately lazy middle-aged man with a full stomach would do.

It is warm, clear and remarkably tranquil as I pass back into the parish boundary after finding the last parking space in a very full layby. The sun lights up the canopy of two ancient ash trees that look like they've been pollarded a few years ago, slender branches now growing out of the tops of thick knotted trunks. Half a kilometre up the tarmac track, past rolling fields of wheat to my left and the hidden splendour of a manor house to my right, only the tall stone chimneys visible, the building I've travelled to meet comes into view. The fields that surround it were sown at the turn of the century using a local wildflower mix collected from the ancient hay meadows I visited last week, and although many of the fussier species did not survive, a good few have flourished and it is still a rich scene, with flower-strewn grassland contrasting with the uniform glaucous green of the wheat fields beyond.

I pass by a moat that is wide and long and brim-full. It is a peaceful sight and satisfies a subconscious desire to never be too far from water. I think anyone who has grown up by the sea and then moved inland probably has a similar outlook. Sycamore and beech planted on raised banks filter sunlight into shallow depths that are in places dominated by broad pondweed leaves. This aquatic plant is flowering in profusion, with hundreds of slender stems breaking the surface, each five or six centimetres tall, scattered angled light turning their colour from greens and browns to oranges and reds.

I walk along a recently mown path that snakes through the meadow, the fresh aroma of cuttings still hanging in the air, on towards solid stone faces of equal length that join to form a formidable Greek cross. The shape of this magnificent yet unfinished summer lodge, commissioned in the late 16th century by Thomas Tresham, former owner of the nearby manor house and fervent Catholic, rather blatantly symbolised a celebration of his faith at a time when Queen Elizabeth I was more than a little anxious about the Catholic threat posed by Spain. She had stopped worrying about her cousin, Mary Queen of Scots,[10] by the time the building revealed its form. Tresham was clearly a man of strong principles, and by refusing to renounce or even conceal his religious allegiance, his fortune was significantly

---

[10] Mary was beheaded at Fotheringhay Castle in 1587, located about 15 miles north-east of our parish.

depleted by a series of punishing fines. He was perhaps fortunate to retain his head. The building might still have been completed if it wasn't for the predilections of his two sons and a series of unfortunate events. His eldest, Francis, was a member of a group of provincial Catholics who planned the famously unsuccessful Gunpowder Plot of 1605. Francis escaped the fate of many of his conspirators,[11] but met an early death in prison from natural causes in the same year. Just for good measure, his traitorous head was decapitated post mortem, shoved on a spike and displayed to the public, just in case they hadn't got the message. Thomas also died in 1605, leaving his land and what remained of his fortune to his youngest son, Lewis, who proceeded to spend little time in frittering away what remained of the family's wealth. Despite such setbacks, Tresham's monument has remained miraculously intact, thanks in part to its relative isolation in the landscape, but mainly because of its acquisition by the National Trust in 1922.

As I stand and admire the clean lines and bold symmetry of such a historic building, the setting sun passes beams through stone frames that have never reflected back the light. A brilliant orange, black and blue small tortoiseshell butterfly basks on honey-coloured stone, drawing my attention to graffiti that is centuries old, the letters W.B. neatly carved and sharing space with the crude outline of a bird, perhaps a raven. I place my palm against the warm limestone and travel back in time. Or I would have, but for being suddenly aware of

---

[11] They were hanged, drawn and quartered, and their remains displayed around England in a very successful PR campaign to deter others who might be thinking about blowing up the Monarch.

a large group of photographers gathering on one of the spiral earthen mounds that looks down on this structure. The photography club, to which the cars that fill the layby must belong, seem like a friendly bunch but are not particularly happy with my presence in their photos, and so I exit stage left and wander east a short distance, past skylarks piercing the air, until I reach nearby woodland. The scents once inside are of a damp, hanging, heady blend of climbing roses, flowering privet, spindle, elder and dogwood. There are undertones of ride-edge grassland cluttered with the yellow-green umbels of wild parsnip, pink-tinged valerian, the scrambling yellows of meadow vetchling and agrimony, all bottled up under a full canopy. Every so often tree cover gives way to blocks of open pasture and as it does so the complex perfume evaporates into an increasingly chilly night air.

Across one such pasture a pink full moon is rising, sitting at almost exactly the same point above the horizon as the retiring sun it faces. The wind, imperceptible for the last two hours, momentarily picks up, rustling the tops of oak, ash and aspen. Blackbirds serenade the moon, first to rise and last to bed.

I walk on until I meet the next expanse of woodland and a wide ride, the rhythm of each footstep counting a slow second. I am aware that I am drifting further and further in the opposite direction to my car, and have to force myself to break my steady forward motion. By the time I return to the stone monument it is past ten o'clock. The full moon, now a pale yellow, is becoming brighter and whiter as it continues on its curve, touching the tip of a large oak that flanks the stone edifice. A female tawny owl serenades the scene. The photographers have gone, picture-postcard sunset snaps taken, leaving me alone with Tresham's ghost bathed in brilliant moonlight.

27th June

As I'm drinking my morning coffee, looking out at the garden with bleary eyes, a juvenile jackdaw that is close to full size but still with patches of downy grey feathers shuffles along the top of our garden fence. Like a novice tightrope walker, it wobbles a little with each sideways step, gingerly inching its way along the ledge, eventually reaching the relative stability of a square fence post. Balance practice over, the bird swoops down to begin methodically stalking the lawn in search of food.

In the small pocket park next to our house, jackdaws nest in pine and sycamore, sharing the space with bulkier carrion crows and rooks. Jackdaws are handsome birds up close, with piercing ice-blue irises, a short beak and glossy black plumage interrupted by a silvery sheen covering its nape. In flight they emit sharp, yapping calls and in the evening when coming in to roost, they tumble together to perform spectacular aerobatics, hundreds of birds moving haphazardly around each other, filling the sky. A flock of jackdaws, known as a 'clattering', is well named.

Unique among the crow family, jackdaws choose to nest in tree hollows, and as they cannot excavate their own cavities they have to compete for a home in a finite market. Consequently, it is not at all uncommon to see adult birds dropping sticks down uncapped chimney stacks and then diving in, head first, to begin the construction of their nest. As a chimney is too narrow for the jackdaw to spread its wings, they have to crawl up the stack to exit, one foot straddling either side, heads popping out like Victorian chimney sweeps. When we first moved into our house, on more than one occasion the echo of a jackdaw's call would resound around the living room and I would open a metal plate on the side of the chimney breast to find a nest mid-construction, penetrating blue eyes staring back at me. Last spring my youngest daughter told me about a scratching noise in her room. I feared the worst and checked for the telltale signs of rodents. Thankfully there were no dark pellets or gnawed skirting boards to be seen, but the next morning the same complaint was issued, this time a little more forcefully. Apparently, the scratching was coming from her free-standing wardrobe. I walked slowly up the stairs, teasing her about C.S. Lewis books and what might be inside, and opened the wardrobe door to be met by an adult jackdaw perched nonchalantly on the clothes rail. I still don't know how it got in there.

These remarkable birds are capable of recognising individual people, can respond to human expressions, will share information about the best spots for finding food with other jackdaws, and are able to rapidly learn new skills. To top it off, recent research has shown that jackdaws use their bright eyes to communicate with each other; prior to this study only primates had been proven to use their eyes as a means of communication between members of the same species. And they devour the slugs that would otherwise munch my hostas.

What's not to like?

3rd July

Five magnificent veteran lime trees tower above a sheep-grazed field that rests between the main street cutting through the village and the Anglican church. They were planted more than 150 years ago by unknown hands, sourced from foreign lands for their ornamental beauty. In many countries, including our own until fairly recently, limes are referred to as linden trees. I much prefer this name, deriving from the Old English 'lind', meaning lenient or soft, a reference to its malleable timber which was, and I assume still is, highly prized by wood turners, furniture makers and sculptors.

The pasture they dominate is currently home to six impressive rams, all broad heads and oversized testicles, dozing in the shade the limes provide. The tops of the trees are pollarded every ten years or so, with the intervening growth cut back to the same point at which it was chopped off the last time pruning took place. Pollarding can extend the natural lifespan of a mature lime tree considerably, and though it looks like a fairly brutal practice immediately after the works are completed, dark-brown branches are soon filled with lop-sided heart-shaped leaves, and it only takes a couple of years for the trees to regain the shape and size of canopies past.

The lime flowers are clustered together in bunches of eight or nine, each inflorescence attached to a light-green canoe-shaped papery bract, which contrasts with dark-green leaves to produce a variegated effect when the tree is viewed from a distance. Though each pale-yellow flower measures only a centimetre across, the total number on each tree must run into the tens of thousands, loading the air with a sweet perfume that hits me long before I reach them. The powerful odour they broadcast is irresistible to insect life, attracting huge swarms of bees, flies, wasps and beetles of all shapes and sizes. Standing underneath a tree, the noise they create is disconcertingly loud, like a buzzing power line, branches alive with energy and frenzied movement.

Some of the smallest insects savour the sweet surfaces of the lime's leaves, made sticky by copious amounts of honeydew produced by aphids after they have mainlined mouth parts into leaf veins and fed on phloem fluid. These tiny aphids can be found on the surfaces of most leaves, and are a feast for ladybirds, who graze at their leisure. The more obvious bumbling bees and wasps flit from flower to flower, gorging on nectar available in overwhelming quantities. It's an all-you-can-eat feast, but it can be a fatal attraction for some. For over a century there have been anecdotal reports of dead bumblebees under lime trees. At first it was thought that the bees might not be dead but rather very, very full and in a kind of food coma, which I can certainly relate to. But recent studies suggest that this mysterious phenomenon might be linked to the relatively low sugar content the flowers offer (surprising for something so sweet smelling), combined with small quantities of caffeine present in the nectar. Whilst this ingredient will not poison the bee, it seems that it might enhance the bee's memory and its association with food, and so occasionally affect its judgement about where to forage. This might ultimately lead to a bee overvaluing the lime tree's nectar, preferring it over other more nutritious options nearby. In extreme cases, the junkie bee might continue to return to the tree even when the flowers are almost completely depleted, meaning that they will use up all their energy in the hope of one more sweet fix. Whilst this is a sad end for the confused bee, the vast majority of local insect life, and the vast majority of bees, benefit greatly from this flowering event, and from the presence of the trees in general. And happily, the ground beneath the limes is currently littered only with a sprinkling of sheep shit.

6th July

Walking up to the woods in the late morning, it strikes me on the way that many of the plants just coming into flower are, literally, in a purple patch. Freshly opened common mallow mixes with field scabious and the elegant blooms of meadow cranesbill, filling out the verges. The margins of arable fields are scattered with perfumed powder-puffs of creeping thistle and leggy black horehound. Common knapweed and selfheal stand out along ride edges, tufted vetch scrambles over grasses and thorns. In very broad terms, these colour combinations contrast with spring, when whites and yellows tend to be most obvious. I've casually wondered from time to time if there is any real pattern to the seasons, flower colour and invertebrate phenology, with certain colours attracting certain insects, or groups of insects, but there again such ad hoc observations might just be due to the size or abundance of certain plants at certain times of the year, or any other of a large number of confounding factors. Still, the thought again keeps me occupied and before I know it, I'm past the twisting masses of seeding oilseed rape fields and into the woodland.

Along open rides impressive black and marmalade-banded hornets are on the prowl, whilst the silhouettes of dragonflies patrol the space above. Ringlet butterflies, at just as much risk from these predators as are small flies, midges and mosquitoes, briefly land to be admired, showing off the reason for their common name, their wings adorned with small circles, each with a pale outer ring and a jet-black inner boasting a white central dot. These particular individuals appear to have only recently emerged from their chrysalides and sport luxurious silken wings the colour of dark chocolate.

Speckled woods and slightly tatty meadow browns flick over tall grasses and herbs, feeding on bramble flowers, sharing the pollen with spotted longhorn beetles that whirr like mini gyrocopters from flower to flower, then up into the honeysuckled scrubland edge. Bright orange skippers, commas and wonderfully fresh red admirals, seemingly always in a rush, dart and dash over scalloped clearings. Purple hairstreaks flutter down from oak canopies to feed on privet blossoms, their metallic colours flashing and changing with angle and light. But these are not the purple butterflies I'm looking for, even if they are a pleasure to spot. I'm on a treasure hunt to search for one of our largest and most elusive butterflies, an obsession for some, a butterfly that would not look out of place in the sultry tropics of the southern hemisphere.

We are fortunate to have ancient woodland within the parish that is tailor-made for purple emperors. An abundance of sallow provides ample food for their caterpillars, who after munching on the willows' leaves for most of the autumn then overwinter on silk pads they construct and attach to the surface of a twig or bud. They emerge from slumber in early spring, just as the buds are starting to expand, and rather particularly then choose a specific leaf to rest on, leaving it uneaten and commuting to feed, returning to base when they have completed their meal.

By this stage the larvae are a beautiful bright-green colour with several faint yellow stripes along their sides which match perfectly the pale veins of the sallow leaf. When finally ready to pupate, a caterpillar will travel to the underside of its chosen leaf and spend a couple of days building a pad of silk from which the pupa will then be suspended. A silken stalk is then spun and securely attached, and the well-fed caterpillar points downwards to begin its incredible transformation. Hopefully emerging about now.

It is not at all guaranteed that I'll see any emperors today, at least at ground level. They are strong fliers and spend most of their time high up in the canopy. In fact, the females rarely venture down to ground level, but it is the males that I'm really after, as only they display the colour of the season. It is often easier at this time of the year to find the butterfly by first looking for small groups of people. And almost straightaway, along a narrow ride at right angles to the main track, I spot three folk kneeling as if in prayer, with large camera lenses pointing to the ground.

Avid emperor hunters will employ all sorts of techniques to lure the butterfly down. A popular trick is to smear onto the ground rancid liquid concoctions containing mashed-up shrimps, which the butterfly seems powerless to resist. Urination is also used as a lure, as are all manner of rotting fruits. It is only a slight exaggeration to say that by the end of the flight season some areas can resemble the trampled detritus left over by a travelling fruit & veg market, or a vegan-themed music festival.

The butterfly I'm studying is settled on the middle of the track, feeding on bare and slightly damp earth, its faintly luminous proboscis, the colour of cheap chip shop mushy peas, unfurled and probing the ground. Even when closed, the undersides of its wings are beautifully intricate, shades of light greys and rusty orange, black markings and white streaks, but every so often the wings flick open to beat off flies, probably attracted to the same source of nutrition. As they catch the sun, brown wings intersected with white bands are hit by light that refracts from the structures of microscopic scales to produce the most brilliant, breathtaking iridescent purple sheen. Although 'purple' doesn't really do the colour justice. To my eye it is a brilliant ultramarine, more specifically a 'Klein blue' for those with a fondness for 1950's art.[12]

By now the people who had attracted my attention to this butterfly have moved on to try to find other

---

[12] Specifically, *IKB 79* by Yves Klein, produced in 1959 as one of nearly 200 blue monochrome paintings

specimens, so I have the scene to myself. As soon as the emperor is focused on fuelling up for an afternoon of flight it is possible to get very close, and I am allowed as long as I want to take photos, even though I must have accumulated hundreds over the years. After taking what I consider to be my best shot yet (almost certainly to be superseded by a better photo next year), I sit down next to the feeding butterfly and eat my packed lunch, admiring its colours and form. The male will soon take to the canopy, perhaps congregating with others around a 'master tree', often an oak, typically found at a high point in the wood where they will hope to intercept passing females. The same trees are used year after year, but their location is a closely guarded secret, and I have yet to find one.

When he was younger, my dog would accompany me on summer walks up to the wood at this time of the year. He has always been a placid companion but on one fateful stroll, and after failing to see the elusive butterfly, we were on our way out of the woods when he suddenly leapt, snapping something out of the air. I took the object out of his mouth and held it in the palm of my hand, wings flashing purple in the sun. It is the only butterfly that he has caught in eleven years, the only time he has even attempted such a feat. The one silver lining was that it made a good show-and-tell exhibit for my youngest daughter at primary school the following day. Or at least it did for the few minutes before the teacher considered it to be a risk to the health of the class. I partially blame myself, as the week before I had given her a dead pipistrelle bat contained in a clear plastic container to show to her friends, which did not amuse the teacher.

I've trekked up to the woods in the hope of seeing a purple emperor most years over the past twenty and they never fail to impress, the hundredth sighting just as thrilling as the first. It is not simply the beautiful colours, size and relative rarity of the butterfly that makes an emperor hunt such a pleasurable and rewarding experience. Even when I don't spot one there are a multitude of other things to admire, and on a still summer's day with the occasional mewing of a buzzard in a woodland heavy with the scent of privet and honeysuckle, there is no better place to be.

9th July

It is just past ten o'clock on a mild, tranquil evening as I approach a road verge leading out of the village. I'm here to hopefully find one of the more remarkable sights within walking distance, one to rival the purple emperor. Concealed amongst the vergeside vegetation there should be small beetles that, if you can find them during the day, appear entirely unremarkable. Many have spent the past three years as larvae, feeding mainly on a diet of snails, but for a few weeks in summer they mature into adults, forgo the gastropods and instead direct their energy into one all-consuming purpose – finding a mate.

It feels and probably looks a bit strange searching for something in the dusk, and it takes a while for my eyes to adjust. The light is a soft blue-grey that blurs the definitions of trees, merges fields with hedgerows, the landscape all clumps and blocks and wonky lines as darkness gradually descends. But out of this increasingly uniform scene something other than the stars and the waxing moon is bucking the trend, become stronger not fainter. Thinly scattered throughout the grassy verge, hovering 30 cm or so above the ground, shining globes begin to appear. The beetles are here, and they are transformed.

Two thick bands of luminous green, and at the tip two more pin-pricks of bioluminescence which look like tiny eyes, glow on the last sections of an abdomen which is turned upwards, slowly waggling back and forth. A female glow worm is clinging to a blade, looking more alien caterpillar than beetle, and certainly not very worm-like. She is lighting up, advertising her presence to males that, unlike the females, do not glow but do have wings and large, photosensitive eyes. The ethereal glow emanating from each female is now by far the brightest natural light as the stars become hidden by cloud, which turns out to hold rain. I can hear the drops pattering on leaves before I feel them but it is a brief, light shower and does not seem to deter the glow worms. The pockmarked ground, still warm, raises the smell of damp vegetation and tarmac.

We are fortunate to have glow worms here. Their national distribution broadly mirrors chalk and limestone geology, and we are on the edge of a band of oolitic limestone formed during the Jurassic period about 200 million years ago. It also helps that there is flower-rich roadside grassland that provides a ready supply of slugs and snails. The phenomenon here does not quite compare, admittedly, with the spectacular 'glow worm' caves of New Zealand that I visited when very young, but it is a rather unfair comparison. For a start they are not the same species, or even genus – the Kiwi creatures are actually fungus gnats, though basing a niche but no doubt fairly lucrative tourist industry around the words 'fungus gnats' would no doubt prove challenging. There is, however, something deeply exciting, especially in the late evening when so much is unseen, about finding such a wildly unusual creature displaying in the English countryside, a landscape renowned for its understated tones. The siren light they emit is surprisingly strong and by 11pm, in the shorter turf, the glow is visible from the opposite side of the road, multiple luminescent marbles sprinkled thinly throughout the sward. I count 38 females in total. Perhaps their presence would become a bit more normalised over time if there were thousands present, but I doubt it.

I noticed earlier in the day that the grassland in the margin between the crop that lies on the opposite side to the road verge and hedge was unexpectedly good, possibly relict vegetation that somehow escaped the very modern management of the arable field. Sure enough, several glow worms are here too, one on the precipice between grass and crop, and one actually clinging on amongst the barley. I would never have imagined that an area regularly cleansed with herbicide and pesticides could be home, at least temporarily, to such an extraordinary animal.

Walking further along the margin, eyes to the ground, a strange high-pitched noise starts up, somewhere between a rasp and a scream. At first it seems to be coming from the hedge, but as I get closer, I pinpoint the sound to a large ash tree. The sound abruptly stops as I approach, which is not a little unnerving, and then a few seconds later a barn owl takes off, the screeching noise following a ghostly form as it flies directly over my head, across the barley field and out of sight, its call still audible but becoming fainter, until I'm standing in silence.

I wander happily back to the road verge, senses heightened in a darkness that we are hard wired to avoid, trespassing into a world for which our vision is poorly suited. My hunt is made slightly more challenging by the occasional car hurtling past, lights blazing, but searching for wildlife at night adds a certain novelty and excitement that outweighs the perils associated with a speeding lump of metal. I share the night with the blur of moth wings and the chirping of crickets, occasional far-off yelps of foxes, tawny owls calling back and forth, the hoarse barking of deer, bats patrolling overhead, faint crackling sounds coming from the hedgerows and strange, sudden, unidentified noises which sometimes seem alarmingly close. What the driver of the car and their passengers thought of me as I appeared unexpectedly in their headlights, I cannot guess. Perhaps they paid me no mind at all, although I like to think that if they could see what I am seeing, they would be just as amazed at the light show they have unknowingly driven past at speed.

12th July

A rustling sound, followed by the slow parting of barley stems only three metres or so away, reveals not a muntjac, or a pet cat, but the head and long tawny-coloured ears of a brown hare, cognac flecked in the early evening light. The countryside here is well suited to the hare, a mixture of cereal crops, wide grassy margins, cattle-grazed pasture and thick hedgerows. The hare seems momentarily oblivious to my presence and for a few seconds it is possible to admire the velvety appearance of its coat, the long, black-tipped ears and large, amber-coloured eyes. Its demeanour changes suddenly when my dog, who has been plodding alongside me on an evening stroll across the back fields, decides to take an interest. Initially indecisive, caught between the urge to flee or to hide, it chooses to lie low for a few seconds, ears and body flat to the ground, well concealed within the crop, but then suddenly it bolts, scattering the barley in bending, narrow lines, jinking and zig-zagging to safety. Hares can, apparently, run at speeds of up to 40 mph, whilst my dog might hit a top speed of a-bit-faster-than-ponderous. It needn't have worried about being caught, although given its lapse in alertness, the hare might not be so lucky if a nearby fox chances upon it.

27th July

A few weeks in remote corners of Scotland catching up with old friends and wandering among majestic scenery has provided the perfect formula for a good dose of the holiday blues. A day of trawling through endless emails on my return to work does not help. By early evening I'm in a foul mood and no use to anyone, and so step outside to try to acclimatise to a clear, uncluttered horizon. I dig into my pockets and find a bent sprig of pine, cup it in my hands and inhale the fresh memories of woods dripping with lichens, giant boulders and fallen trunks softened by thick carpets of colourful moss, of vertiginous waterfalls and twisting streams flowing over smooth rocks balancing dippers and wagtails.

Considering my relatively short absence away from the village, I'm amazed at how much has changed. Meadow brown butterflies have given way to freshly emerged orange and coffee-brown gatekeepers. They patrol hedgerows now full with the white gramophone-shaped flowers of hedge bindweed. Pink and white-striped petals of the much smaller field bindweed weave through grassy roadside banks, their candy colours climbing up tall, straw-brown stems of spent grasses, whilst black and yellow-striped cinnabar moth caterpillars feast on common ragwort, methodically stripping their hosts bare. Crickets and grasshoppers compose the song of high summer.

The luminous-pink spikes of red valerian that adorned stone walls by the Catholic church are now exposed skeletons. It is warm and close, the sun dithering behind high cloud. Squabbling flocks of house martins appear as clustered specks high above, ensnaring invisible food. A red kite looks ragged as it drifts overhead, feathers moulted after rearing young. I think of my balding head and my daughters soon to fly the nest. As I pass the church towards the humpback bridge, fields of golden oats stand ripe and ready for harvest, as do the barley fields, noticeable in the distance as large ochre polygons. On the far side of the river the flood meadow has been cut and baled, the curlews long departed. A sea of fruiting docks flow through the land left fallow, their rusting spires set off by stately light-green burdocks.

Silver streaks of mugwort light up the verges. Stands of nettles that a couple of weeks ago would sting my shins are now approaching shoulder height and hold dangling cords of inconspicuous pale-green flowers that, when disturbed, produce fine clouds of pollen that hang in the air. Great willowherb, covered in straggly hairs and pleasingly soft to the touch, rivals the nettles for height but boasts more obvious blooms, each one pink with a white cross-shaped stigma bending down over the lower petals. Rings of tiny parma violet flowers peek out from conical teasel heads. Tangles of flowering bramble are alive with iridescent flies and beetles, honeybees, wasps, hoverflies and bumblebees, the latter's legs heavy with yellow blobs of pollen.

The first flush of hogweed is on the turn, their umbrella heads now full of flat, broad, translucent seeds sporting dark lines painted on each face, the pattern revealed when I hold one up against the early evening light. Spindly cow parsley stalks persist nearby, their fruiting heads still clasping a few narrow, blackened, tubular seeds. Hedge parsley, the last of the 'big three' common umbellifers to flower, has just come into bloom. It is an elegant plant, considerably smaller and neater that the hogweed and cow parsley, although its basic structure is the same, with each individual having a mass of tiny but perfectly formed bright white flowers stitched together to form an umbrella flowerhead held above coarsely serrated, elongated leaves.

Mature ash trees that have, so far, escaped the destructive effects of the pernicious die-back fungus are in peak condition, their canopies full and lush, their curved branches a resting station for song thrushes, woodpeckers, blackbirds and dragonflies. The familiar spiky casings enclosing horse chestnut conkers have appeared where not so long ago there were gaudy candelabra flower spikes. The aroma of thousands of lime flowers that still filled the air as I left for Scotland has been lost, replaced by pea-sized fruits covered in a fine down.

By the riverside, the first sweet stands of Himalayan balsam lure hoverflies and honeybees that disappear into the mouths of large pink bonnets and emerge with yellow backs. Seed heads have already begun to form and dangle next to the flowers, their explosive potential soon to be released. Banded demoiselles bask on the balsam's broad leaves and below them the river flows, its level so low that it is possible to see where the footings of the bridge meet gravels and silt. Collapsed stems of bulrush and long linear strands of a water-crowfoot waggle in the current.

In sheltered, deeper inlets the first golden-yellow waterlily flowers have poked their heads above broad pads resting on the surface, while their submerged cabbage-like leaves lurk below. White froths of meadowsweet brighten dark green banks in the distance. A light wind cools my face in sporadic pulses, gently bending the odd branch and patch of grass. It is all a far cry from raised bogs, brilliant-red sundews, dazzling white beaches, inquisitive seals, steep corries and broad-winged eagles. But after a couple of hours of walking, pausing, observing, the yearning for mountains and lochsides fades, gently replaced by the subtle beauty and depth of this familiar landscape, a place where I have established deep roots.

3rd August

Sporadic downpours over the past few days, followed by unbroken skies, have meant that although the barley is ripe for harvesting, their bent heads obligingly awaiting the guillotine, it is still a bit too wet for the chop. Massed hordes of adult and juvenile swallows twitter, swoop and skim over spared whiskered heads crackling under a warming sun, the birds feasting on flies, exposing cream bellies as they turn for another pass. There are views of the river and a mix of black, red and white cattle beyond, grazing in a pleasingly neat, coordinated line spanning the width of the flood meadow.

Further on, the grasslands are buzzing with grasshoppers, potential food for hovering kestrels with still heads. Southern hawker dragonflies cruise the tall reedy margins buffering the river. A narrowboat passes behind the reeds, unseen but not unheard, the retro sounds of a 1980's earworm blasting out. I reach the shade of a narrow path above wet woodland that leads to the north-eastern edge of the village, past scattered knee-high runs of hedge parsley, the yellow heads of cat's-ear arising on thin stiff stems, basking peacock butterflies and gatekeepers lazily skipping over brambles. Perennial sowthistle, one of my favourite summer flowers, is in peak condition, resembling a slimmed-down version of a sunflower. Its stems and yellow heads are covered in stalked glandular hairs, each sticky microbead contributing to a halo around the plant that glistens when backlit by the sun. But one plant in particular turns the head.

Many of the wild flowers in our countryside are poisonous, or are at least unpleasant to taste, whether it be to insects, deer, rabbits, or to us. It is evolutionary common sense; if you're not delicious, you are less likely to be eaten. In a very few cases the toxins contained within the leaves or the seeds are particularly harmful to humans and have developed names in folklore appropriate to their properties. *Atropa belladonna*, otherwise known as deadly nightshade, is one such species. It is not particularly uncommon in the south of England in places where the underlying geology is either chalk or limestone, but it is a rare plant here, sitting as we do on the tips of the fingers of the limestone bands. The path where it is found, and which I'm currently walking along, is kept open using mowing and brush cutting equipment by a small group of volunteers living in the village, of which I am one. There is a strong incentive for keeping the way clear; it is the swiftest walking route to the nearest pub.

The nightshade is a tall, bushy herb with broad, spear-shaped leaves that have impressed veins curling from the centre to the edge. The whole plant is, like the sowthistle, covered in tiny glandular hairs, including its unusual liver-coloured bell-shaped flowers. Later in the summer, large black shiny seeds will form, bearing an uncanny resemblance to the chocolate minstrels that I used to devour on my way home from school. But these seeds are not for eating. Although all parts of the plant contain alkaloids to be avoided, each seed contains on average 2mg of atropine (hence the Latin name *Atropa*), and if eaten can lead to hallucinations,[13] impaired memory and disorientation, and if you're really unlucky can result in depression and circulatory collapse, followed by death from respiratory failure. Shakespeare's famously unfortunate Juliet apparently ate a handful of deadly nightshade berries following the rather farcical miscommunication with Romeo. No mobile phones back then. Atropine does, however, have some positive medicinal benefits, as long as it is prescribed by a qualified practitioner in the appropriate dose. Amongst other things, it can reduce salivation during surgery, and dilate pupils to help ophthalmologists to get a good view of the retina during an eye exam.[14] But it can also conjure up the Devil, if you believe the scribes who noted its use in soupy witches' brews from the Middle Ages. All things considered it's probably best to simply admire the plant, as I do, without being tempted to ingest any part of it, no matter how delicious the seeds appear to a hungry rambler.

The dog and I head back and loop around to meet the trickling brook. The grass bordering the shallows is short enough to see grasshoppers springing just ahead of each footstep, and something else is moving too.

---

[13] Deadly nightshade is called 'loco weed' in some South American countries

[14] In 16th-century Italy, women applied eye drops prepared from deadly nightshade to dilate their pupils, a look which was considered desirable at the time. History does not tell us if men also risked applying a toxin which would inevitably be ingested, although it's probably fair to assume that the social pressures of the time went in one direction.

A few tiny froglets, only a couple of centimetres long, crawl and hop and stumble near to the fenceline. The dog sniffs but seems more curious than hungry. I manage to catch one and, holding it in cupped hands, have a peek. It is a dark mossy green colour with a faint yellow line running along its eyes and sides. The body is smooth and teardrop-shaped with just a hint of a vestigial tail. This is a perilous time for froglets. They would make tasty tapas for a rook, heron or fox. I put it back in the grass bordering the brook, and wish it luck.

7th August

An evening stroll with the dog along a regular route passes a cereal field next to the deconsecrated church at the edge of the village, almost within sight of home. From a field entrance by the roadside, neat rows of barley straw run down towards the brook, the open waters of the gravel pits visible in the distance. The harvest is underway, but a cacophonous noise puncturing the still evening air, drifting up from the bottom of the freshly cropped fields, is not mechanical. I can just make out huge flocks of brown birds, and as the walk has just begun, I run back home to fetch my binoculars, the dog not best pleased to have his routine interrupted.

When I return, I can see more clearly what I could hear from a distance. An enormous gathering of starling-sized birds is having a party, packing out three thick power lines that run across the width of the field, the cables supported by four evenly spaced telegraph poles. There must be more than one thousand, but they are not the familiar colours of adult starlings and as a novice birdwatcher I am momentarily stumped as to what they are. Walking down as far as I dare, following the freshly cut stubble next to the gathered straw, I get a better view, my brain whirrs and clicks, and it dawns on me that the aggregation is comprised exclusively of juvenile starlings. Most unlike the dark glossy plumage of the adults, these youngsters display a mish-mash of mottled grey-brown and cream colours.

As I watch, more juveniles flood in until they are perched wing against wing. Every available space is filled, including the stanchions of the telegraph poles, so the only choice for the recent arrivals is to move further along to vacant lines in the adjacent field, until there are birds three deep stretching for perhaps half a kilometre. I am familiar with seeing large flocks of starlings in the autumn and winter, but this is the first time I have noticed such a massive flock in the summer months. In my excitement I walk just a bit closer to get a better view, and as I do so the inevitable happens. The birds lift as one enormous flock in the direction of the gravel pits, leaving power lines to bounce and wobble for a good minute afterwards, relieved of the combined weight of such a spectacular sight.

12th August

Harvest is in full swing, and there is an underlying sense of urgency around the village. Tractors, trailers and combines are an almost ubiquitous sight in fields and along country roads, backing up cars resigned to follow in their lumbering wake. In the barley fields close to home, a faded yellow New Holland TX34 combine harvester, its name proudly displayed in a weathered red stripe across its belly, roams slowly, relentlessly onwards, pausing only to turn at the end of each run to line up the next. Built in the early 1990s, it is a wonderfully angular machine, a world away from the GPS-controlled self-steering modern monsters that cut twice as wide and so eat up a field in half the time. The TX34 has two massive front wheels, a couple of almost comically small rear wheels which steer the vehicle, and is operated from within a large glass cockpit that juts out angularly from the body, suspended above and just behind the cutting blades and header to allow for a clear line of sight.

The mechanics of harvesting are relatively straightforward, even if the technology behind it has become increasingly complex. A spinning hexagonal reel on the header catches the barley, which is cut with knives attached to a spinning auger that feeds the material into a central point. From there the barley passes into the stomach of the combine where threshing takes place, the grain dropping with gravity through a series of augers and sieves, eventually collecting in a large tank behind the cockpit. The straw is separated early on and excreted out of the rear end, generating great clouds of dust and depositing a deep trail of debris which will later be baled and eventually used as bedding for livestock in the winter months, or even for food in drought years when hay prices can be desperately expensive. A tractor with trailer attached waits nearby until the combine's stomach is full. The grain is then regurgitated through a long tube that swings out from the side of the machine, its load spilling into the trailer, generating more thick beige clouds as it pours out, filling the pan to the brim.

As I watch the TX34 steadily making its way across a field that is now half crop and half crew-cut, Orthoptera chirp from the sidelines, hidden within long grasses spared from the blades, their songs providing top notes to the deep droning of the machine. Insects are busy on pink bramble flowers, oblivious to the carnage taking place a few metres in front of them. Buzzards cut low, ready to pick off mice, voles, partridges, even young hares that are driven out of the diminishing crop by the combine's blades, only to be exposed suddenly to a new danger. Red kites roam overhead, waiting to pick off what didn't make it out of the field in one piece, or does not now have the benefit of a dense crop to hide within.

The sun begins to dip below the clouds, spilling out columns of crepuscular rays across a hazy white-ribbed sky, but fading light does not stop play. Powerful headlights will cut through the darkness, creating a halo around the combine, from a distance bringing to mind images of a submersible exploring the ocean depths.

17th August

Sitting in the garden, drinking my first coffee of the morning and attempting to recover from a rare but particularly acute whisky hangover, I'm shaken out of my torpor by a large insect landing on the glass table where my mug is perched. On first sight it would seem to have the colouration and size of a hornet, complete with a bright yellow stripe running between its large brown eyes. I am fond of hornets, but not so much when I am in a fragile state and not at my sharpest. Still, it doesn't seem to be intent on harm and I can't summon up the energy to move. An enforced stillness lends time for a closer inspection, and it becomes clear that the hornet is not quite as large as it should be. The body is too broad, has darker shades of yellow, and then it dawns on me that there is no sign of a sting. A fumbling search using my phone identifies this rather spectacular individual as a hornet mimic hoverfly, which seems to sum it up quite nicely. This fly was considered to be an extreme rarity in the past, colonising England as late as the 1940s, but as the climate has warmed so numbers have increased and the species has moved northwards.

After a second and third coffee, and as I gradually come around, I notice the dog has taken an interest in something on the lawn. He seems to want to eat whatever the mystery object is but nervously backs away each time his nose gets close to the grass. I shuffle over, gently nudge him out of the way and see a very impressive caterpillar that at first twitches from side to side and then, astonishingly, rears up like a mini cobra, ready to attack. I can see why the dog was apprehensive. The caterpillar has tiny black stumpy legs, a small white-tipped spine at one end of its khaki-green body, four enlarged 'eyes' at the other end that are actually not eyes at all but glistening warning spots, and what seems to be a large 'nose'. This last feature, with a bit of imagination, could be perceived as a trunk and gives its identity away. But for a bleary start to my morning and the need for fresh air, I would certainly have missed both this elephant hawk moth caterpillar, which will in the spring metamorphose into an even more dramatic creature with wonderfully patterned wings of ginger, pink and green, and the hornet mimic hoverfly. That is, in any event, my excuse for the excesses of the night before, and is already more than enough excitement for one lazy day.

21st August

As our largest land predator with a keen sense of smell and razor-sharp claws, badgers preferred meal is earthworms, but small mammals[15] are also fair game and, at this time of the year, so are other less obvious prey. Ambling along a grassland path at first light, I almost stumble into a freshly dug ankle-breaker hole with a neat circular entrance. Inside are the remains of what must have been quite a sizeable wasp nest, the fragile grey construction now reduced to shattered fragments covering the soil close to a metre below the surface, where a few wasps still lurk. Angry wasps, no doubt.

In order to take these insects on, the reward really does have to be worth it. In this case, it is a well-stocked supply of juicy protein-laden larvae. Most animals would not survive digging up and feasting on an active nest, but badgers are shielded by a thick wiry coat which they fluff up for added protection when attacked, although the nose of this particular badger must surely be hurting this morning. Nests only seem to be plundered in late summer, probably because this is the time when worker, queen and drone grubs are all present and so the rewards are at their greatest. It must have been a fierce battle to witness, the tenacious badger tearing through the top of the nest and layers beneath, the wasps desperately swarming and stinging. The aftermath has revealed the merest fraction of the abundance of life unseen in the soil beneath my feet. And it is a reminder, if one was needed, to keep a respectful distance from a badger.

---

[15] Including, unfortunately, hedgehogs

27th August

Small talk about the weather is never far from the lips of dog walkers, and for a few days folk have been grumbling about an autumnal presence. It is hard to disagree, as much as I'd like to. The mornings are noticeably colder, although the hope remains that this is just a blip, that summer still has a time to run. But juvenile swallows, told from the adults by the lack of red on the head, are massing in the fields, hunting in packs, gathering together on high wires, signalling the beginning of the end of their stay in the village. The thick smell of cropped cereals hangs in the air, loading the skies, microscopic fragments of barley causing my eyes to itch. The light has gone by eight.

Berries are ripening, reflected in the violet-coloured bird droppings that splatter pavements and the tops of wooden gates, seemingly always at the spot when my hand reaches to push them open. The first bitter-tasting crab apples litter the ground. Much of the vegetation looks a bit tired, ragged or spent after a busy season, although late summer flowers still brighten up corners and verges, hogweed is having a second wind, and along the riverbanks and streamsides, Himalayan balsam, an annual plant invisible for much of the year, flows amongst nettles, white bindweed trumpets and stately angelica plants, forming dense pink patches of sickly sweet scented bonnets. Close by, stands of common reed at last display their dark purple plumes, bending in the breeze like exotic tail feathers.

Such signs of summer's end, or at least the beginning of the end, prompt me to explore the woodland to investigate whether colours have begun to be revealed under fading green leaves, but the hedges on the cycle up show no imminent signs of turning. As I reach the brow of the hill that leads into the woods a distracting, insistent high-pitched call reaches me from the bare branches of a dead elm jutting out from an oak-filled periphery. I dismount from the bike, legs a little weary after the ride up, and hurriedly dig out my binoculars just in time to catch the briefest glimpse of what is probably a young hobby as it lifts off in pursuit of a harassed parent, both birds disappearing into the depths beyond. I stand and wait in the hope that they will return to the same spot so that I can get a better look. A couple of jays fly up into the recently vacated elm. I can just make out the hobby's faint call somewhere off in the distance.

Sometimes it pays to be indecisive, because as I loiter in the margin of the ripe wheat crop abutting the woodland edge, vacillating about whether to stay or to move on, amidst the whirring of crickets there's a rustling sound about a metre away. Then an erratic movement of grass stems within rank vegetation dotted with yellow ragwort, daisy-like mayweed flowers, violet thistles and purple knapweed, all mingling with a smattering of stiff wheat heads. I stand as still as I can, and a tiny outline, then the ink-black eyes, pale-ginger body and long smooth prehensile tail of a harvest mouse appears. It is almost within touching distance, nibbling on an ear of wheat, replicating the pose of grainy photos from childhood books. Almost immediately it spots me and scurries to vanish into the dense vegetation, its heart no doubt beating almost as fast as mine. It is difficult to describe the elation that comes with such a totally unexpected sighting. I could search all year and not find a harvest mouse, but though this is a chance encounter, sometimes you make your own luck. Now that the mouse is aware of my presence, I doubt that I will see it again but I wait for a while, stock still, just in case.

After fifteen minutes or so of happily replaying the harvest mouse memory reel, there is still no sign of the hobbies (or the mouse) so I walk my bike across to the opposite side of the field in search of the birds, along tractor lines that have over numerous runs throughout the spring and summer created bare ground within the full crop. As I approach the area where the falcons appeared to last call, the clouds part and the sun strikes the wheat which almost instantly begins to sizzle, ripe ears drying with the sudden rise in temperature. It becomes so warm that I have to remove a layer, back to a T-shirt. It feels like high summer again. So much for the early morning pessimism. As I near the end of the makeshift track, two adult fallow and a young fawn dawdle out of the wood. They don't notice me for a few seconds, then perform a comical double take as my presence is registered. I stand and watch them bounce through the wheat, heads appearing rhythmically above the crop, a heat haze shimmering between us.

There is a convenient gap through the hedge-lined bank in front of me, probably created and kept open by regular deer sorties. I emerge on the other side, and a hobby flashes past. This time I get a better view of its long, curved, pointed wings propelling it over a pigeon-battered maize crop, and out of sight. In its place, two ravens loom towards me and the wood, emitting guttural croaks as they pass low over ash and oak. At the point when I am ready to enter the woods, my original mission for the day, it is almost time to head back home. But the call of the raven lures me in. I regret not bringing my lunch, a schoolboy error.

Inside, the wood is looking relatively fresh when compared with the exposed landscape that falls beyond the reach of the canopy's shade. Meandering paths are mostly dry and hard, but some sections are muddy and churned, speckled with the small lime-green leaves of water-starworts, a memory of waterlogged conditions earlier in the year. The colourful ground flora of spring past is now dominated by the browning tones of grasses, of graceful tufts of hair-grass, upright spikes of bearded couch, swathes of false brome and elongated culms of hairy brome, a woodland specialist, four feet tall and bending under the weight of its spikelets. Most pleasing of all is a large patch of wood barley, a sign of quality and an excellent indicator of ancient woodland. Most of the grasses in front of me would not look out of place in a Chelsea show garden, though a designer could never hope to replicate such natural complexity. Late-flowering plants such as corn mint, a speciality of the rides around here, stand out not only for the colour that they add, with whorls of mauve petals wrapped around leaf axils, but most particularly for the knockout minty aroma they emit when accidentally stepped on. Congregating above the mint and the rides, migrant hawker dragonflies are plentiful, released to hunt by a warm midday sun, the clicking of their wings audible as they weave and turn. Fresh broods of red admirals and speckled woods find sun traps cast by dappled light to bask and feed.

I could stay here all afternoon, but hunger pangs get the better of me and so, reluctantly, I start for home, emerging into a bright warm afternoon. Views of the valley and village stretch out below. Kites call overhead, and then a sharper, snappier noise stops me in my tracks. I rest my bike against a barbed fence and scan the area. A pigeon flies a decoy run and then I spot it, a hobby cutting over the treetops, hugging the space between woodland and pasture where its food flies unawares. As the hobby turns to pass, its body reflects bright sunlight, turning its form a silvery grey. The falcon, which resembles from a distance a chunky, more powerful version of a swift, suddenly draws in its sickle-shaped wings and drops, stooping, accelerating at incredible speed before pulling up at the last second to skim a couple of metres above the grass, hugging the fenceline, performing razor-sharp aerobatics with micro flicks of its outstretched wings as it manoeuvres and zeroes in on its prey, rising and dipping, tracking the outrageous dexterity of a dragonfly.

The hobby disappears from sight behind a line of blackthorn and after a few seconds emerges, gliding above the grass and a woodland backdrop, its head bent towards bright yellow talons, devouring its prey on the wing. Through my binoculars I get wonderful views of the bird, its white collar and cheeks and contrasting black Mexican moustache clearly visible. It is also apparent that the bird lacks the peachy-red thighs, or 'trousers', of a mature adult, marking this out as a juvenile, which is great news. I stay rooted to the spot, watching the hobby hunt and feed and rest, picking out the details of its yellow and black hooked bill, its leathered talons, the intricate patterning of its underbelly, marvelling at its effortless agility. I recall my chance meeting with a birder when I disturbed him by the wet woodland and the river margin, and text him to confirm the successful rearing of young. He responds almost immediately, very pleased. Earlier in the day I messaged my eldest to say that I was off out to the woods for an hour or so. She said she'd see me in four. She knows me too well.

2nd September

Large congregations of swallows and house martins, often comprising many hundreds, have started to pass through the village, massed silhouettes clustering, weaving, racing against ashen clouds. For a brief time, their calls fill the land, a maze of twittering, clattering activity as they fuel up for their southern adventure. And just as abruptly as they appear, they are gone, leaving behind a silent, mournful sky.

7th September

Defining the seasons using time spans set to the first of the month is useful if you're a climatologist who requires consistency from year to year in order to examine trends. It is certainly far less confounding than relying on partitioning time through the observation of natural indicators of change: daylength, temperature, the position of the stars in the sky, the life cycles of plants and animals. Walking through the back fields in the early afternoon on my way down to the river, the shining curvature of smooth scarlet hawthorn fruits and spherical deep-burgundy berries dripping from elders hint that autumn is turning the page, though the burning sensation on the back of my neck feels like a defiant last stand for summer.

Brambles now hold a succession of green, rosy and black berries, the latter ripe and easily plucked, although the fruits are in direct sunlight and the taste is a bit like drinking warm, overly diluted Ribena, rather than the cool sweet sensation I was hoping for. Silk-soft seed heads of spear and musk thistles are erupting in ultra-slow motion, their compact powder puffs spreading and separating, incrementally releasing tiny seeds that each sprout a spray of fine white filaments to aid their dispersal. Most only travel a short distance before being trapped on the surfaces of nearby plants, but some will escape their clutches and sail away on updraughts.

I reach the ancient water meadow, the first time I have been down here since it was cut by blades and later grazed by cattle. The grassland has a slight spring to it, uniformly short save for a smattering of rushes that have already begun to recover their forms, slender glaucous stems brushing my knees as I move across the lower lying areas. Large white butterflies with sooty-edged wings pause to feed on yellow cat's-ear flowers standing out in a sea of green. Craneflies wander awkwardly through the vegetation, their long legs snagging every so often on stunted blades.

An elliptical depression sitting in the distance is currently bone dry and coloured a pure white with a mass of mayweed flowers, neatly demarcating an area where water once ponded and curlews probed for food. In the middle distance a couple of moorhens nod across the river, swimming towards tall willowherbs which are holding long narrow pods unzipping to reveal their white webs of feathery seeds. There is an overwhelming impression of stillness in this heat, the only sounds the occasional yapping of far-off jackdaws, the rapid rub of grasshopper legs and a cooling breeze that picks up every now and then, rustling the liminal vegetation. I turn to start for home and a cool drink, hugging the shadows of the hedgerows, and hear a low humming sound. Cruising slowly down the river, three rosehip-red human heads come into view, their boat lost in the screen of reeds, suncream seemingly forgotten.

After a couple of glasses of water in the relative cool of my kitchen, acting on impulse I pack a towel and trunks and head back out to a path that leads to my favourite spot for swimming, the entrance hidden amongst willows. There is no gentle gradient here, just a ledge and then deep water, so the best and indeed only course of action is to plunge in, bypassing the creeping agony of slow immersion into cold water. And it is bloody cold. After a few strokes my body sort of acclimatises and I begin to take in the scene; straight ahead, downstream, is a flat-topped medieval church built on a steep knoll bulging above the river. Alder and willow blanket the bank to my left. To my right is a large expanse of flood meadow, largely hidden by tall reeds and seeding iris. Upstream the river arcs around the water meadow and alder woodland.

I breaststroke my way to the opposite bank where the curlew meadow stretches into the distance. My feet blindly feel for shallow ground, finding first submerged waterlily leaves, then a fine silt which I sink into up to my shins. Perched half out of the river, balanced against the weak current by performing vaguely circular motions with my hands, I turn towards the sun, welcoming its warmth. The water is a turbid murky green, but after a minute of standing fairly still it begins to settle and clear. Fish begin to materialise in front of me, ranging in size from the length of my little finger to longer than my outstretched hand. Brilliant-blue dragonflies zip overhead as I push out and into the middle of the river. I turn to rest on my back, arms outstretched, a cornflower-blue sky meeting my gaze, and allow the current to carry me gently downstream.

Getting out is the tricky bit. I have to manoeuvre my right leg to an angle of 90 degrees, find a firm spot in the muddy bankside and push up and out, grabbing roots with my left hand whilst avoiding nettles, hoisting my left knee onto dry ground and, when firmly anchored, pivot my body up and out. I am glad that this is a secluded spot. Drying off, Loudon Wainwright's swimming song jumps into my head, with lyrics I haven't heard or thought of for the better part of twenty years. I step into sandals with soles that soon become soggy, gather my belongings and head for home. My arms and legs are speckled with tiny lime-green duckweed fronds, stubbornly clinging to my skin but gradually released as they are baked dry by the last of the summer sun.

14th September

It is curiously easy to miss the large horse chestnut tree that sits rather incongruously on its own in the middle of a large arable field overlooking the river. It should stick out like a sore thumb but somehow manages to blend in from most angles against a background of riverbank willows and hedgerows, only becoming obvious when viewed directly against the wash of green in the distance. For much of the year the chestnut stands in solitude but today, in between the harvesting of one crop and the sowing of another, it is possible to walk through the stubble which crunches underfoot and admire the view that the tree has year-round. I pass a large pile of greying badger dung deposited neatly in a small depression as I make my way across, blackberries still identifiable in the droppings, and sit down on a thick woody finger that has ploughed its own furrow. I rest my back against a generous trunk.

The footpath and village lie hidden behind me, the landscape ahead falling to meet the river, a flat expanse of flood meadow and undulating arable fields beyond. Down to my right in a dip where the river periodically encroaches, a large green triangular area stands out from the ochre stubble. This corner is sown each year with a mixture of herbs and grasses that hold their seeds into the autumn and winter months, providing food for the birds and compensating to some extent for the efficiency of combines that seldom leave gleanings behind. Below and to my left, canopies of towering willows blend to create, on a still day, a billowing olive-green wall stretching the length of the bank as it curves towards the west. On a day such as today, however, their long flexible branches arch back to reveal the undersides of countless thousands of lanceolate leaves, their pewter tones flashing as bright sunlight appears out of racing clouds. Strong gusts shake the branches and leaves of the chestnut above. Sitting in a field in the middle of England, miles from the coast, this is the closest I can get to experiencing a seascape, white horses racing, the noise above like breaking waves.

22nd September

It is the equinox, one of two days in the year when the northern and southern hemispheres are illuminated equally, day and night shared evenly. Into a setting sun I walk to the pasture that joins onto our back garden, note the spot that should precisely mark due west, then briefly nip home to fetch a jacket, the sudden drop in temperature taking me by surprise. In a darkening sky, washed-out blues and violets radiate above a vanished sun. It is not the sunset that I've popped outside to see, though, picturesque as it is.

I make my way to a spot by the fenceline where there is a lengthy gap in the hedgerow that allows uninterrupted views across the neighbouring stubble fields, out to distant poplars and willows lining the twisting river. It is perfectly still. As I wait in the half-light, a female tawny owl responds to the familiar 'twit-twoo' hoot of the male with her clear sharp 'kee-wik' calls. Her delivery is surprisingly loud, and I trace it to an ash tree only fifty metres or so away, though the owl remains formless within the canopy's cloak. A clattering of jackdaws passes overhead, on towards their roost, sweeping across Venus, the first bright speck of light in a developing night sky. The tall grass by my feet rustles as something small passes through, probably a mouse or a vole, or a rat. Two bats zip by at head height, tracing the line of the field boundary. All the while I scan the eastern horizon.

In most respects the harvest moon is like any other full moon, but as there is a shorter rising time between sunset and its appearance it results in fewer hours of darkness, and a clear sky tonight means that there could be dusk-till-dawn light. Gone are the days when farmers depended on this moon to guide their work, but it retains a deep romance and symbolism that reaches far beyond utilitarian function.

Earlier in the day I looked up the estimated time of the moonrise, but as the minutes tick on without a sign and the cold starts to seep through my coat, I decide to stretch my legs and stroll down to a lower field to try a different angle. The light has almost gone and the occasional rabbit burrow makes it increasingly tricky to walk with any confidence. As I reach an open gateway and turn the corner, back into open ground, the horizon glows faintly, like a distant metropolis. As the luminosity intensifies, a clean bright orange arc breaks the skyline, gradually rising and filling out to form a vast and perfect circle surrounded by a hazy halo of rippling tangerine. It looks for all the world like a sunrise.

I am always slightly taken aback, when paying close attention, at how quickly our most prominent natural satellite rises and arcs into the night sky. After fifteen minutes or so the moon has emerged from a veil of low cloud and changed from deep orange to gold. As it continues to climb, the colour slowly alters again to a disc of bright yellow, the orange influence fading. By the time the moon has topped the silhouettes of ash and oak it is an intensely bright flashlight white, picking out features in the landscape: tufts of grass, anthills, undulating ridges in the grassland. I look directly up for the first time in a while and after my eyes adjust, I'm able to join the dots of Cassiopeia and Pegasus. Behind me the Plough takes shape. I wonder how many countless others are enjoying this moment, this unifying constant.

After a while my nose begins to numb. I head back through the field gate, soon spotting the upstairs windows of our house glowing in the distance. I pass the spot where I stood earlier to wait for the moon to appear and pause to take a few largely unsatisfactory photos with my phone.

As I line up the final shot there is a crunching, rustling sound straight ahead, very close, moving through the stubble, not the light touch of a rodent this time but clearly the heft of a bulkier animal. I tap the torch icon on my phone and point it in the general direction of the noise. I had assumed that I would see a fox, or more likely one of the many muntjac deer that have become a common sight. Instead, in the spotlight, a black and white striped head with shining eyes stares back at me, almost within touching distance. I think I am as surprised as the badger, and we meet each other's gaze for a second or two before it scuttles off to begin its nightly search for food, the harvest moon helping to guide its way.

28th September

Sparrows love an unkempt piece of land. On a walk to the village shop I am guaranteed to be greeted by a loud chorus of cheeps and chirrups on passing a large patch of unruly brambles that has been left to fill out an abandoned gateway by the side of a large stone barn. What is to me an impenetrable mass of thorns is a playground for the birds. They dive in and out of the looping, arching tangle of thorns, occasionally resting in plain sight so that I can admire their chunky form. Sparrows are sometimes dismissed as having a dull, rather scruffy appearance, a lazy description perhaps based on an association with scruffy places.

The adult male that has perched a few feet from my own is anything but dull. Its wings are a warm chestnut brown streaked with black and a hint of white. The crown and nape are a slate grey that would be the envy of posh paint aficionados, the sides of its head a reddish brown, and a black streak by the eye moves down to colour the throat and form a prominent black bib on a dusky-grey belly. Admittedly, the adult females and juveniles that live in this colony are not quite as spectacular in comparison, being a more uniform sandy colour with brown and grey streaks on the back and wings, but they too have their own understated splendour. The sparrow's gregariousness and familiarity never fail to brighten my day.

5th October

The green lane that leads up to the wood has become a bit of a mudfest after recent torrential rain. I am trying my best to dodge the many puddles that have formed, the weather catching me off guard, my wellington boots left languishing in a cupboard at home. The dog casually strides along, muddy feet and fur not his concern. A perfectly clear, pale-blue sky washes overhead but the legacy of the overnight downpour, not heard or seen by me as I soundly slept, is not only underfoot. As the morning sun rises above thick hedgerows lining both sides of the lane, the eastern-facing boundary begins to sparkle as light strikes raindrops still trapped in a mass of foliage, snaking with gravity to collect, hang and fall from the tips of leaves and branches. Mixed among the shrubs and ash trees in the drying hedge, one plant stands out at this time of year. It is more commonly found on old walls around the village but here it is concealing trunks and spilling into crimson haws, dull purple sloes, ripe blackberries and shining red hips.

Ivy is a familiar sight, instantly recognisable to genus but surprisingly tricky if you wander down the niche path of attempting to identify the multitude of different species and varieties that grow wild, each displaying their own subtle variations. Some folk still hang onto the notion that ivy is a thug, slowly strangling the life out of trees, but in fact ivy is harmless, has its own root system and so doesn't rely on the tree for nutrients or water. And it is fantastic for wildlife. In early spring the dense evergreen foliage presents nesting opportunities for robins, dunnocks, blackbirds and wrens. It offers camouflage for bat roosting sites and, in the winter months, a home for hibernating insects. The leaves are also a foodplant for a number of butterfly and moth caterpillars, and no doubt also many insects which I have yet to encounter or learn about.

It is the flowers, however, that are currently providing the interest. Trees and the tops of the hedgerow nearby are wreathed in a mass of countless thousands of greenish-yellow clusters that teem with insects dancing around each other, greedily searching out nectar. Each cluster contains upwards of thirty tiny flowers, held on short stalks that extend out from the woody tips of adult plants. Each flower emanates from a central point, and holds five pale-green petals and five anthers sticking out around a short single central style. The flowers are said to have a sweet honey-like aroma, but smell is a subjective sense and I have read one memorable description that defines it as a combination of semen, sewage, and rotting laundry detergent. To my nose, they have an odd but rather appealing musty perfume. Perhaps I am just lacking in imagination.

The globular form of the floral arrangement is usually referred to as 'umbrella-shaped', but up close it reminds me more of a full pincushion, or those spiky naval mines that pop up in old war films, only spotted when inches away from detonation and disaster. As most other plants in the vicinity have long gone to seed, the late-flowering ivy has a near monopoly on attracting pollinators. It is clearly a successful strategy and a striking sight in early autumn. I spot honeybees, wasps, tiny flies and hoverflies, bumblebees, a spectacular hornet, numerous beetles, some impossibly fresh red admiral butterflies and quite a few ivy bees. The latter insect times its emergence to coincide with the appearance of ivy flowers, which seems like a sensible move, although there is certainly more than enough to go around. The ivy bee looks a bit like a honeybee but is distinguished by a thorax covered in ginger hairs and distinct black and buff stripes on its abdomen. It would have been a remarkable find only a few years ago but they have spread rapidly since naturally colonising our shores at the start of the millennium, and there are tens of them buzzing away in front of me. Though a welcome and rather handsome addition to our fauna, the ivy bee, like any other invertebrate, depends on external heat to raise its body temperature, and so it follows that its presence here in the early autumn is perhaps double edged, evidence of a warming world.

11th October

About fifty sheep have appeared in the back field. Not earth-shattering news, but I am at first a bit perplexed as to why they are here as the grass seems well grazed. I put the dog on a short lead, offer a 'thank you, ladies' as they move away from the worn grassy path formed by years of following in each other's footsteps, and almost instantly amend my statement, apologising to the large ram that reluctantly steps aside. This would explain the return of the sheep, and the lambs that will be skipping through the pastures about five months from now. Some of the sheep have coloured backsides, stained by the ram as he goes about his business, blue chalk strapped to his undercarriage. A field of blue arses is good news for the farmer, and evidence of the tireless effort put in by the randy ram.

It is not just the livestock that are starting afresh. Passing the rusting crown of a large sycamore and entering the adjacent field, glinting blades are turning over and transforming cereal stubbles into deep brown ribbons, each pass of the plough dragging gulls and kites in its wake, erasing at a stroke the evidence of a season's work, preparing the ground for the next. A few fields have already passed this stage, their memory wiped clean, soils broken down and rolled into a level bed ready for the drill. Tracks left by wandering fox, deer, and hare stroll out from the grassy margins, shallow footprints mapping recent journeys on an otherwise blank canvas.

The acrid smell of a smouldering bonfire drifts from the corner of a large garden to meet me. A sharp mewing call gives away buzzard silhouettes cutting high overhead. In the hedgeline, brown catkins hanging from planted birch trees disintegrate into fine confetti with a satisfying crumble as I strip them with thumb and forefinger. Brambles are dripping with ripe and ripening fruits. Scarlet and crimson haws mix with bunches of translucent guelder rose berries, bearing a tantalising resemblance to the sweet glacé cherries that perch on iced Bakewell tarts. The sun still warms in sheltered spots, tempting the removal of layers, but my mind is soon changed as I move beyond the thick buffer and face a cold northerly whipping over exposed fields.

I walk down the hill and over a narrow bridge that crosses the brook, where a weathered laminated A4 note nailed to the kissing gate in April still alerts dog walkers, in fairly stark terms, to the presence of lambs. Though the alders that line the riverside show no obvious signs of change, I soon spot a few fallen ash leaves on the ground and as I continue my regular stroll around the perimeter of the grassland, the dog lost in a world of fresh scents to be investigated, it gradually dawns on me that there are fallen leaves everywhere, some resting by fruiting mushrooms: common puffballs, pleated inkcaps, yellow fieldcaps, grey mottlegills and a few blackening waxcaps displaying various shades of orange, yellow and charcoal. Whilst at a casual glance most trees and shrubs still appear to be clinging on to their summer layers, it soon becomes apparent that the pure dark greens of hawthorns have mellowed in tone. Many of the ash trees appear quite jaundiced, and some elders and elms that fill sections of hedgerows are easily picked out from a distance, the former as fawn chunks, the latter as flamboyant yellow flames, the first bright sparks of autumnal colour that will soon sweep through the lines.

Nearing the village, drifts of sepia, russet and chocolate brown leaves are accumulating along the base of a long fenceline, a few piles so deep that they are asking to be kicked. In the paddock next to the church, canopies of regal lime trees, not so long ago humming with life, are gradually fading to their winter form, long bracts brittle and rusting, some falling to earth with their hard spherical fruits still intact. Several of the leaves at head height display prominent black veins standing out on mottled yellow, amber and black surfaces. A couple have the empty cases of ladybird pupae attached to their surfaces. Adult beetles rest nearby, perhaps the same ones that have emerged from these hollow shells. They display their own autumnal colours. One has glossy black wing casings with two bright red splodges, the other is a lighter grey with orange markings set out in a wonky grid formation. Both are harlequin ladybirds, a variable-looking species and a recent arrival to this country. In just a few decades it has developed the formidable reputation as the most invasive ladybird species on earth, although I suspect it has little competition for that title. Like all ladybirds, I find them strikingly beautiful and charismatic, but from the perspective of our native species they aren't quite so attractive, as the harlequin is relatively large and has a voracious appetite. Not only do they compete for finite food resources, but they can, on occasion, also eat the larvae of 'our' ladybirds.

We are often quick to demonise foreign plants or animals that outcompete native flora or fauna, labelling them as unwanted invasive 'aliens', but it is not the harlequin's fault that it has ended up in this country, and they do not live out their life harbouring some malevolent hidden agenda. Native to an area that stretches from Kazakhstan to Japan, the harlequin was intentionally introduced into several European countries in the 1980s as a biological control for aphids. It eventually found its way to our shores, perhaps hitchhiking in vehicles, or maybe in luggage, or perhaps on the wind if we want to be absolved of any blame. Love them or loathe them, they are here to stay. And at least they eat a lot of aphids.

18th October

As chlorophyll breaks down all around us, plants offer a fleeting revelation of the bonfire of chemicals – flavonols, carotenoids and anthocyanins – that lie hidden under verdant greens for much of the year. Depending on conditions, a vast spectrum of colours might stick around for a couple of months or so, but whatever the weather, branches will soon be bare and the landscape changed completely for another six months. Maybe it is because I am at an age when the phrase 'the autumn of your years' is beginning to strike more deeply that it once did, but I find autumnal days that boast intensely saturated blue skies to be some of the most beautiful. And today is one of those days.

I make my way to the woodland, a natural destination in the circumstances. I have no real plan, although I do carry a field guide to mushrooms in my bag. When I was about nine years old, for one late summer and autumn I became obsessed with fungi. It was the bright red cap of the fly agaric that hooked me, that and being told it was poisonous, music to the ears of a child with an overactive imagination. Though my attention abruptly switched to a different passion the following year – I think it was Panini football stickers – and my interest buried, it was never truly lost and in recent years I've occasionally attempted to identify some of these incredible organisms that pop up close to home, neither plant nor animal but something in between.

I am a little hot and out of breath by the time I have cycled up to reach the edge of the wood, and find it a relief to step into shadows and dappled light. The occasional light gust of wind gently releases streams of leaves, in amongst them a red admiral butterfly which I mistake for just another colourful leaf until it darts off, giving itself away by flying against the breeze. Chestnut-brown acorns are easily plucked from their cups. Some oak leaves display bulging crimson growths, to the extent that from a distance the tree seems to have an outbreak of chickenpox. These growths, or 'galls', are formed by tiny wasp species, and turning a leaf over I see that another, the spangle gall wasp, has been busy creating small spherical constructions that resemble press studs, or miniature flying saucers, each one containing a single larva which will emerge as an adult in the spring.

I soon spot my first mushroom, and it's a beauty, about six centimetres tall, with a broad dark-fawn cap, the margins of which have turned violet, this colour seeping down into the rusty-brown stipe.[16] It has a beautiful veil covering the gills, as fine as spiders' silk. I break off a bit of the cap and the flesh soon turns a violet colour, and there is also purple staining on the stipe where I picked it. I can't immediately identify the fungus using my book, decide that it is probably a bruising webcap, and pop a specimen in my container for closer examination when I get home.

Resting my bike by the path, I walk very slowly, head down, scanning the ground, great tits sending out alarm calls, a raven calling close by. After a few minutes a phalanx of beige mushrooms appears out of the leaf mould, sticking up from a rotting moss-covered branch. They have small, conical caps with subtle striations, more

---

[16] The 'stalk' of the mushroom

obvious when held up to the light, and beautiful, delicate gills narrowly attached to the stipe, which is long, thin, and very stiff, pinging back when flicked. I'm fairly sure what they are and bend back the stipe of one to breaking point. An audible fracture confirms it as a snapping bonnet. Wandering the few metres back to the path, I see there are several more fungi that I missed earlier, including an impressive vermilion beefsteak fungus the width of my hand, growing out from the base of an oak. In the past, and if I were a wood turner, this tree would have been of significant value, as the beefsteak causes the timber of the infected oak to turn a highly prized rich-brown colour.

I am too much of a novice to be able to pick out promising areas where the glamour fungi might lurk, but my brain slowly begins to filter out the confusing fug of grasses, brambles and fallen leaves. I'm wandering blindly in the hope of finding something, going on a treasure hunt without a map or knowing what the treasure might be, but then it is not exactly hard graft drifting slowly through a woodland illuminated by funnelled shards of light, accompanied by birdsong and the occasional barking of fallow deer. I reach a section of old conifer plantings where the soils are slightly changed and the ground littered with cones resembling pangolin armour, and am greeted by a golden fungus rising out of exposed trailing mossy roots. Surrounded by earthy browns and greens, though it is only a few centimetres tall, it is almost impossible to miss. Its form is unlike the standard image of a mushroom, and looks instead more like a branching coral, about the length of my little finger and rather rubbery and greasy to the touch. According to my book, this last character distinguishes it from other similar species as a yellow stagshorn. The texture reminds me of small toys I had as a child that I would throw against windows and then watch slowly 'walk' down the glass. As I am studying the stagshorn, my nose close to the ground, a hornet buzzes past my face, taking me by surprise and causing a few choice expletives to follow the insect, reverberating into the depths of the wood.

Walking deeper into an area of tightly packed conifers, there are bright orange false chanterelles, some lovely bluish-grey brackets, a false saffron milkcap which exudes brilliant orange latex from its gills, and a couple of wonderfully delicate scarlet bonnets with translucent red caps on stipes only a couple of centimetres tall. Maybe best of all, curving out of a rotting log are a couple of smooth chestnut-brown caps and pale stipes with shallow brown vertical ridges. I turn one over to examine the gills, see instead a soft cushion made up of thousands of tightly-packed tubes rather than the usual thin papery lines, and recognise it as a bolete. As someone partial to all food, I know that boletes are sought after and can be very tasty. Some, however, are not. After a few minutes of flicking through my book, I turn back to the mushroom and see that the stipe has turned shades of red and blue, and where I touched the pale-lemon underside my fingerprints have left a perfect dark blue imprint. These characters combine to most likely identify this mushroom as a bay bolete, supposedly delicious, and as a bonus the accompanying text states that it is 'usually free of maggots', which is good news, but does leave an air of suspicion hanging over some of the other edible fungi ripe for the picking.

I am not quite daft enough to think that, as a complete beginner, I can identify accurately every mushroom I have found, and I certainly would not eat any without first seeking an expert second opinion. Still, it is nice to think that I can perhaps recognise a few, at least to the correct family. I am beginning to get my eye in, but truth be told as I start to spot more where once there was just leaf litter, it all becomes a bit overwhelming. I pause to stand in a sunlit patch and as the warmth starts to seep through my jumper, I think back to when I first began to try to identify the flowers in our local wood, over forty years ago. The fastest way to become confused and disenchanted is to attempt to identify everything at once, and I decide to be satisfied with being able to recognise just a few each time I go out and to try to cement the names and features in my memory bank for the next foray, so that I might be able to build on what I've learnt. There are no short cuts. It takes a lot of time, patience, practice, aptitude and failure to become proficient in just about anything: 1.5 hours down, 9,998.5 to go, if you believe the rather arbitrary number of hours it is said to take to become an expert in any particular subject. I look in the container that has several fungi to check and see gold, custard, deep orange, yellow, chestnut, red, white, crimson, violet, and feel myself becoming hooked.

24th October

Although it is late October, the hedges behind our house are still full of fat blackberries ripe for the picking. With the sun shining, I wander out carrying a couple of plastic tubs to forage the filling for tonight's pudding. I am just underway as a near neighbour walks past, warning me rather gruffly that blackberries plucked at this time of the year are the Devil's berries. She has a point, assuming the Devil prefers the soft, slightly mouldy blackberries retained on spiny arms that I have already examined and rejected. But there has been little rain lately and this, combined with relatively warm days, means that plenty remain firm and sweet. I'm sure he wouldn't mind if I took a few of these.

I am very choosy at first, knowing that the lower field I'm heading towards is always a good bet for a blackberry bonanza. As I reach the open gateway that leads into this field, I see that I'll be sharing my patch with a couple of cows, but they don't seem to mind me being there and after a bit of inquisitive sniffing, they settle back down to tearing and munching the grass. The hedges that surround this rectangular field are about six metres deep and at least four metres tall, and in long sections they rise to over seven or eight metres. The number of different shrubs and trees that grow in a stretch of hedgerow can give a good idea of how old it is, with the rule of thumb being that if there is an average of four woody species in two or three 30m sections of hedge, then this would tend to suggest that the hedge is about 400 years old, although it is important to be aware that this 'formula' can vary by 200 years either way.[17] This method for hedge dating was devised by Dr Max Hooper in the 1970s, a lovely man and brilliant ecologist rarely seen without his Kufi-style hat and who, coincidentally, lived in the village next to ours. There is an average of just over seven species in this stretch, including field maple, dogwood with dark green

---

[17] And very modern hedges tend to be planted with lots of species for the benefit of wildlife, so muck up the rule completely!

leaves rapidly turning a deep burgundy, hazel, buckthorn, elder, blackthorn, hawthorn and spindle. An old and diverse hedge by any standard, quite possibly pre-dating the enclosure of fields that cut up land across the county in the 17th and early 18th centuries, transforming so much of our landscape by dividing large open fields into individually owned plots.

The spindle is a rather nondescript tree for much of the year, tending to be lost amongst the more familiar shrubs, only giving itself away if you happen to examine more closely its paired dark-green leaves, or spot its display of tiny whitish-green flowers in the spring. It becomes quite the exhibitionist in the autumn, though, with a mass of spectacular hot-pink fruits popping out from fading foliage. The shape of the fruit is also unusual, each one having four bulging compartments containing a single seed. The tough pink casing of a few fruits has split open to reveal their shiny, bright-orange seeds hanging by a tiny white thread, so that they dangle and wobble slightly in the breeze. These seeds are sometimes described as resembling popcorn kernels, though to my eye they look exactly like orange Tic Tacs. In a dried and powdered form, the seeds reputedly act as a laxative, although as their ingestion may also lead to liver and kidney damage they are probably best avoided, with a trip to the local chemist the safer option.

I scan the best bramble spots and start to pick, standing on tiptoes, disentangling my arms from sharp thorns for much of the time, the largest and most appealing blackberries seemingly always the highest, just out of reach. Even so, I fill one tub quite quickly. As I begin loading a second, a song thrush with a flawless spotted cream breast briefly appears in front of me, moving within the body of the hedge. As it passes from left to right, out of the corner of my eye I spot a long grey-green blob that registers as being slightly out of place. I turn my attention to the blob, anchored to thick intertwining rose stems weaving up through the guts of the hedge. It is the nest of a long-tailed tit, immaculately camouflaged, an astonishingly beautiful and intricate piece of functional art.

The nest is vaguely bottle-shaped, hence the alternative name for this bird, the 'bottle-tit', but it could just as easily be said to have the shape of a gunpowder pouch that would have been in use several hundred years ago, when the hedge might have harboured the distant ancestors of this year's fledglings. It has a small circular entrance on one side, near to the roof, and is painstakingly constructed in early spring using a recipe of moss, lichen and fine grasses, all held together with gossamer silk collected from spiders' webs. This last ingredient has a famously high tensile strength, often quoted as stronger than steel, and this, together with its inherent flexibility, means that the nest retains its structural integrity but is able expand as the young chicks grow inside. To top it off, the nest is lined with hundreds of feathers, giving the youngsters a cosy, pampered start to life. I have found fallen examples on the ground in the past and still recall how incredibly light and soft they are in the hand. The hedges around here must contain countless nests of many different bird species, but for obvious reasons I rarely see one before branches are bare.

My shadow begins to stretch out across the field, now bathed in a mellow honeysuckle light, and I turn for home with two takeaway plastic containers brimming with berries, fingers stained purple, the smell of warm crumble only a few hours away.

27th October

The field maple is one of my favourite trees, especially at this time of the year when its leaves turn shades of butter and gold, orange and rusting reds. Like the sycamore, or indeed any maple, it produces familiar elongated papery 'wings', each containing a single seed. These structures are more formally known as samaras. Two bullet-shaped nutlets (the seeds) are initially fused together, the papery wings that surround them spreading outwards to form the shape of a propeller. As the nutlets ripen they separate from each other along a neat split down the centre. At the moment most of the samaras are still green, but some have turned red or light brown at the margins, and this change of colour reveals more clearly the network of finely curved veins that cover the wings. These give the structure greater rigidity, in much the same way as the complex network of veins function on the wings of a dragonfly. When the samara eventually detaches to fall from the tree, this venation will help to slow the rate of descent and so increase the chances that it might be caught on a gust of wind and be dispersed further away from the parent tree. And the farther away the seed gets from the parent plant, the better in terms of the genetic diversity of future offspring. And, in time, the more field maples to admire.

31st October

Waxcaps belong to one of the more obviously glamorous fungi families, their fruiting bodies popping up at this time of year in an assortment of glowing colours. The best places to find them tend to be old pastures that are cattle- or sheep-grazed and have never been sprayed with herbicide, but such spots are hard to find, and though the water meadows here fit the bill in terms of their soils and history, they are generally far too wet. Away from the fields, however, on slightly higher ground, there is one area in particular where the turf is ancient, well-kept and free of artificial herbicide. And what better place to search for waxcaps on this day than a graveyard?

All Saints' Church is a magnificent building, chiselled into shape by skilled medieval craftsmen using Barnack stone once quarried in nearby Lincolnshire. John Dryden, considered by some scholars to be one of the greatest English poets and playwrights of the 17th century,[18] was born and grew up in the rectory opposite the church, and was christened there. Its imposing square-shaped bell tower, topped off with four long pinnacles pointing skyward from each corner, soars high above all other buildings in the village save for its main competitor for soul saving, St Peter's Church, to which a tall spire was added in the late 14th century, that bit closer to God (and lightning strikes). All Saints' is studded with an amazing array of gargoyles, from weathered winged beasts and contorted faces, to strange birds and bearded satyrs. Standing at the base of the tower and looking up

---

[18] Bear in mind he had some fairly illustrious peers, such as William Shakespeare, John Donne, John Milton and Ben Jonson

at these creations looking down on me, the blue sky is broken up by racing white clouds, creating the illusion of the tower stuck in a loop of the first stages of falling, juddering backwards and forwards. It is an unsettling but oddly compelling experience, a feeling of vertigo with feet planted firmly on the ground.

One glance at the cemetery lawn tells me that I probably won't find what I'm looking for, at least in the large expanse where the graves stand. The grass is long and rank, left uncut for at least the past couple of months by the look of it, for the benefit of other wildlife no doubt but it is not the short turf I was hoping for. The small area of front lawn, however, situated by the roadside where a large war memorial stands, is kept tidy and regularly mown, a more promising hunting ground.

Sure enough, growing out of the mossy sward next to a few prostrate rosettes of hoary plantain, I spot my first snowy waxcaps of the year. Their caps and stipes are smooth and have a waxy feel, as you might expect, and are a pure ivory colour throughout. Turning one over, its paper-thin gills, like most waxcaps, are decurrent, meaning that they continue like a tight corset down the stipe below the point of attachment with the cap. The flowing patterns created by the structures and shapes of the gills are exquisite, with a kind of venetian blind effect produced as the stipe is turned and the angle of light adjusted. But they are first and foremost a functional feature. Millions of microscopic spores are manufactured within the gills[19] of each fruiting body and are catapulted by surface tension to be released on

---

[19] Technically known as lamellae

air currents, although only a tiny fraction will go on to germinate, fuse together and grow into new mycelium. The spores come in a variety of colours, with most shades of white, pink, brown or black, though they can be brilliant oranges, yellows, reds and greens. If you want a glimpse of just how prolific the gills are, take a fresh cap home, place it face down on a sheet of paper, cover it with a glass or a bowl and then lift the cap after a couple of hours. We might not see them as we go about our daily lives, but spores are everywhere, and globally each year many millions of tons are dispersed into the atmosphere. It is estimated that on average we inhale up to ten spores with every breath. The sheer abundance of these particles can even influence the weather, with their moisture-loving nuclei contributing to the formation of water droplets in humid air, and so the creation of clouds, fog and rain.

I continue my search, head down, feeling more than a bit self-conscious stalking around lichen-encrusted rectangles, shields and crosses, and the occasional grave with a fading posy of flowers. There is nothing new to be seen, which is slightly disappointing, though perhaps something other than the undead might rise up from the soils tonight. The dog hasn't had his afternoon walk and the light won't last too much longer, the clocks having turned back last night, so I stroll the few hundred metres home to collect him. We take the side path that leads to the back field and the start of our regular circular route, and as I pass through a wooden gate, I'm astonished to see a troop of waxcaps poking up within the sheep-grazed turf, a couple of metres from the wire fence that marks the end of our garden. I have never considered searching for waxcaps here, mainly because I know that this grassland was sprayed with herbicide in the past, resulting in a rather dull and restricted array of plant life and also, I had incorrectly assumed, a dearth of nice fungi too. Most of the mushrooms have a colour combination of apricot and green covering parts of the stipe and cap, though some are an almost pure bottle-green and all have a smooth, reflective, slimy surface with yellow-green gills underneath. Resembling tiny glass sculptures, they are all one species, the parrot waxcap, and there must be hundreds scattered about. Perhaps this marginal area escaped the sprayer and I have walked blithely past them for multiple autumns. Either that or the field is beginning to recover after regular grazing and an absence of chemicals. It's hard to say; you can only find a fungus when it decides to show itself, and even then, they are easy to miss. I've struck lucky in both my timing and the fact that my search radar is still flickering.

Now fully focused on the job in hand, I soon spot butter waxcaps appearing out of the short turf like tiny golden parasols. A few paces further along, on an almost imperceptible ridge in the pasture, there are a few brain-like specimens of meadow coral, their branching ochre-coloured stems packed closely together, nestled in the grass with snaking yellow clubs poking their waxy tongues out of the soil. I'm still wondering how I could have ever missed these fungi so close to home when, cosseted in a particularly mossy area a couple of paces from where I am kneeling, I see the most obvious of all, six sturdy meadow waxcaps in peak condition, displaying pristine peach caps and wonderfully sinuous cream-coloured gills beneath. It still seems incredible to me that each of the colourful complex shapes and structures that I hold in my hand are constructed entirely from a mass of tightly packed fine threads, often only a cell thick, whilst the main body of the fungus, a branching, fusing network of tubular cells, is hidden beneath my feet, accumulating the resources required to be able to grow and support the fruiting body.

The dog, however, is far from enamoured by my glacial pace. I reason that I can come back after the walk, and we move on. As soon as we are home, I step back out in the half-light to explore the rest of the pasture. Save for a few common mushrooms associated with cow dung, I find precisely nothing. But who knows what might turn up next week, or next year, given different weather conditions? For absence above the surface does not equate to proof of absence beneath when it comes to these marvellous, secretive organisms.

6th November

A thin grey band that was sitting on the horizon when I last looked up from my work has suddenly spread to fill the void, snuffing out the light, roaring on swirling sheets of horizontal rain that begin to batter my office window. A ferocious howling cuts though the house as I watch blurred canopies in the pasture, limbs bending and flailing helplessly, leaves ripped from branches in speeding, swirling ribbons. The dog pushes open my office door with his nose and hides under the desk by my feet, shaking and panting. The neighbour's fence is fractured on the lawn. It feels like the roof above my head might be torn off and swept away. It is not quite the great storm of 1987, when I arrived home to see an oak tree leaning at an angle of 45 degrees, the lower section of the trunk obliterating our front gate, its spreading crown half hidden within my bedroom. But it does bring back the memory. The violence of the storm departs just as abruptly as it arrived, its relentless advance trailing silence and a clear sky. Outside, the road and verges have merged into a deep mess of twigs, branches and fallen autumn colours. I look up, fully expecting to see gaping holes where tiles should be, but all seems miraculously intact.

The same cannot be said for two once-magnificent ash trees that stood near to where I picked blackberries and found the long-tailed tit nest a few weeks ago. Giant arms torn from their bodies lie prostrate on the turf next to headless lichen-encrusted trunks still defiantly rooted in the soil. In the blink of an eye of the storm, the broad familiar silhouettes that softened the horizon and framed sections of the river valley below have been replaced by open vistas and long, fresh, open wounds.

11th November

Our feathered visitors of spring and summer are now a distant memory, but lost sounds have returned to fill the autumn air. The gravel pits and surrounding pastures once again ring to the chiming call of teal, their soft whistling not so long ago drifting across far-off expanses of wetland in northern Eurasia, the same mirrored wings flashing green as they sprung vertically to rise from small pools and remote marshland to begin their south-easterly migration. They share their wintering grounds here with hundreds of wigeon, fellow travellers escaping the cold, harsh Baltic weather. Their high-pitched, drawn-out and rather melancholic whistle, quite different from the teal, can be heard year-round in some of the more northerly locations in Britain, but around here their call signifies shortening days and extra layers. The females are the muted colours of autumn, the drakes picked out from a distance by cream mohicans on chestnut heads.

Away from the gravel pits, heading down the green lane, all puddles and sodden leaves and mud, now more brown than green, different Scandinavian visitors catch my attention. They roam in scattered flocks above hedgerows draped by ivy still flickering with life, where resident goldfinches, greenfinches, yellowhammers and a couple of bullfinches flit and weave. The recent arrivals rise and drift from one side of the lane to the other to pluck soft ripe berries, for a time hidden in borders of gold, vermilion and olive green. Flushed out by my forward motion, their distinctive 'chack-chack' chattering calls retreat a safe distance. This pattern is repeated for a kilometre or so until they peel off to the surrounding fields to hop about searching for worms, snails, grubs and other tasty morsels. It is the first time I've heard fieldfares since they left in late winter, and they are to me the autumnal equivalent of the orange-tip butterfly or the cuckoo in spring, a herald of change.

Fieldfares are a particularly attractive member of the thrush family, and the influx of birds whose calls will fill the landscape for the next five or six months spend the spring and summer in woodland, moorland and open tundra as far away as eastern Siberia. Their colours, however, reflect the current season with a rich chestnut-brown back and wings, a liberally speckled light-ochre breast, light-grey head and rump, and a distinctive long black tail. The redwing, another nomadic thrush escaping the advancing winter in its breeding grounds, often accompanies flocks of fieldfare, although they tend to arrive a bit later, closer to the end of autumn. It helps to see the two birds together to separate them, but once you get your eye in the differences are obvious, the redwing being a much smaller, slightly dumpy bird with a shorter tail and beautiful rusty-red underwings seeping into a mottled cream breast, particularly obvious when the birds are in flight with wings raised against a blue sky. The redwing also has a very different call, more of a thin, drawn-in sibilant 'seep' sound. And if there is still any confusion, it boasts a sleek cream stripe just above its eyes, painted onto a nut-brown crown.

As I move beyond the shelter of the lane, into a more open landscape, and begin the climb up to skirt the boundary of the wood, a large flock of siskin along with the odd redpoll interloper bob over fields with a stop-start whirring of wings. The arc of the sun is noticeably shallower than it was a few months ago, with low angles of light cast over mocha-brown fields, picking out translucent blades of the first flush of winter wheat.

Reaching the brow of the hill, I turn to take in the view. A mile or so into the distance the spire of St Peter's marks out the centre of the village. No roads are visible from my vantage point but a low background hum of traffic is carried on the wind in waves. The landscape running down towards the church, either side of the green lane, is dominated by arable and intersecting hedgerows boasting a few mature broadleaved trees. In the middle distance to my right, a rectangular block of planted woodland sits on the crown of a hill above the crops, out-of-bounds to all but the gamekeeper, his gun, and his pheasants. To my left, a tranquil pastoral scene rolls into the distance, neatly divided up and flecked by the white and brown specks of sheep and cattle. The gravel pits, ancient water meadows and the curve of the river lie hidden in the valley beyond.

Rather than retrace my steps I decide to take a slightly more circuitous route home, walk up to the woodland boundary and then turn at a right angle along the neighbouring arable margin. A tall even-aged stand of black pines with straight grey trunks flanks the land to my right, open vistas are to my left, but ahead of me the edge of a dense sallow thicket blocks the way, its interior swallowing the early afternoon light. Thick wooden fingers engulf the margins, tumbling over a defunct and rusting fenceline. Deciding not to veer off into the crop and risk trampling the young wheat, I scramble on through the sallow in order to reach the connecting path that will carry me back down the hill, and soon find a narrow deer track to follow, hoping that it will not take me in the wrong direction, deeper into the wood. A muntjac barks close by, and as I'm brushing away brittle branches a sunbeam picks out a few glistening silk threads directly in my eyeline. I pause to admire the spider's efforts and more strands begin to appear, until it is gradually apparent that the sallows are loosely stitched together by a complex gossamer maze. It is a bit like a scene in a bank heist film when a combination of smoke and light suddenly reveals an intricate network of laser beams defending the route to the safe. The blur of a tiny spider appears in front of my eyes, abseiling down from the brim of my hat, the Ethan Hunt of the woodland world.

Far from being impossible, the way soon opens up and before long I'm walking down a rutted footpath in the same direction as a small bird that perches from time to time at the top of the thin neat hedge flanking the path. Every so often I get close enough to make out a flicking of wings and what appears to be a russet chest, dark head and white collar, only for it to move on just as I get within range. Forgetting binoculars can be a frustrating business. It's not until I get home and pluck a bird book from the shelf that my brain kicks into gear, and I realise that I was looking at a stonechat, a bird I normally associate with shingle beaches on the east coast, but which is known to roam inland at this time of the year. Another visitor to add to the list, but this time from closer to home. I didn't catch its accent, but if it had sung out, it might have revealed a Norfolk twang.

16th November

As the early morning alarm perseveres, a warm bed can act like a magnet, especially when outside it still appears to be the middle of the night. Add in a bit of driving rain pummelling the windows, and hibernation seems tempting. But on the plus side, having to rise before first light does mean that scenes which might have been slept through in the summer months now unfold at a more sensible hour. If the night has been still and clear, familiar views can be transformed by a mist that generates a blank canvas, earth indivisible from sky save for the floating outlines of a few distant trees and the darting silhouettes of starlings, jackdaws and kites materialising and vanishing in and out of the white void.

This morning, as darkness fades out, I sit and watch a pale turquoise sky give way to shades of pink, tangerine, peach and cream, a hanging wash of pastel tones that gradually transmutes into a mellow low-wattage golden glow as the sun heaves itself above the horizon, brushing the hides of cows wandering across velveteen pastures, their heads down, munching the last of the fresh growth. On mornings such as these, the struggle to surface is soon forgotten.

21st November

It is mid afternoon and the dog has been staring at me intently for the past ten minutes or so, ears pricked, as I tap away on the keyboard. Time for a walk. It is the first time I've had to put on my thick coat since early spring, and in one of the deep pockets I find a half-eaten packet of chocolate biscuits, the kind that are left in B&B rooms next to sachets of coffee and UHT milk. I am tempted to find out if they are still edible. It is fast approaching the time of the year when our appetites increase, stimulated by colder weather that results in a falling body temperature and an innate urge to stay warm. That is my current excuse, in any event.

I have different excuses for other seasons. The colours of the landscape as we make our way down to the river seem to reflect this seasonal need for warm, comforting, calorie-filled sustenance. I look around and see fields, trees and borders in shades of caramel, chocolate tart, lemon cheesecake, cherry pie, plum pudding, toffee fudge, marmalade, butterscotch, honey, pistachio, liquorice. From the depths of my coat, the cellophane wrapping containing one soft bourbon biscuit crinkles between my fingers.

It seems to be a good year for sloes. The yellowing blackthorn hedges are laden with fruits that look a bit like miniature plums but are not at all pleasant to consume. They are rarely taken by birds, not because of the taste but because they are too large. Mice or voles might have a go at tackling a few that have fallen with the leaves. Blackthorn spreads by underground suckering roots so that the thickets massed along the field boundary where I'm wandering could, theoretically, derive from a single clone. In folklore, this shrub was believed to dispel negativity and have powerful protection imbued in its wood, making it the must-have material for wand whittling. The true colour of its bitter-tasting fruits is hidden beneath a powder-fine natural yeast, bestowing a frosted steel-blue veneer. Or, if you follow the folklore route, perhaps this coating denotes the warm breath of a witch imprinted on the sloe's cold surface when in search of the perfect twig. This outer layer is easily and quite satisfactorily wiped clear when handled, revealing a beautiful indigo colour beneath. I roll a plucked sloe between my fingers and think back to when it was hidden within a pure white flower.

The cattle have been taken off the ancient water meadows that join the river, their legacy a liberal scattering of frisbee-shaped pats which will help to feed the soil and next year's grass. By munching down the late-summer growth they have also left behind a short sward which is vital for sustaining the diversity of plant life that has accrued here over the centuries. The ridges and flatter ground are pockmarked with the impressions of heavy hooves, providing space for the potential germination of seeds that have accumulated in the soil over time. The rising water table can be tracked by the appearance of molehills, with mounds of freshly excavated, crumbling earth running in urgent lines from lower-lying areas to higher ground. Furrows are beginning to hold crystal-clear water above saturated clays, and nearly all of them contain one of the rarer plants growing in our area, tubular water-dropwort, which persists throughout the winter months thanks to the presence of antifreeze proteins in its feathery pale-green leaves. On colder days than this the leaves can be seen suspended in ice, much like an insect trapped in amber, though unlike the long-dead insect the plant remains very much alive.

Standing at the river's edge, looking out over an expanse of water meadow meandering into the distance, a large bird the size of a grey heron, unnerved by my presence, rises elegantly from the reed-fringed margins downstream. Long black legs stretch out behind snow-white plumage, a graceful neck and a dagger-like yellow bill. Powerful curved wings beat once a second as it passes low over the water, its reflection almost converging with its body, white tips centimetres from the surface. The majestic great white egret was until recently a rare and exotic visitor to our shores, and until the early 20th century was slaughtered throughout its continental breeding grounds so that fancy hats could be decorated with its long feathers. But greater protection in the last fifty years, resulting in expanding populations, particularly in the Netherlands and France, alongside improved conservation of wetland habitats and warmer winters, have all combined to make these birds a regular sight here in the colder months, wandering north from their southern footholds. In the years to come perhaps a few of these 'ghost herons' will remain to nest in the tall willows that are so abundant in our local landscape, and so grace the spring and summer months too.

The egret flies out of sight, following the course of the river, and I turn to face the sun which is low in the sky, level with my eyes. It throws down a narrow beam that runs the length of the field, and as the dog pauses to lap from a furrow it dawns on me that there is something unusual about the appearance of the pasture within this thin illuminated strip. The grass is shimmering. I crouch down and look along a silver band that runs with the light. It is covered in a fine film of diaphanous silk that stitches together the tips of the grassland. I move a few feet to my left and the line of silk follows, but search where the sun is not directly ahead and there is only grass, the threads invisible. Even now I know they are there and bend down for a closer look, I cannot see them in the shadows. I walk crab-like across the width of the field, squinting into the horizon. The glistening band moves with me, like moonlight striking a dark green sea, and I realise that the entire surface of the pasture is covered in a concealed veil of intricate lacework.

This remarkable scene is the work of perhaps a million tiny moneyspiders, each about half a centimetre long. For a brief time in the autumn, when conditions are just right, the spiders climb to the highest point of their surroundings, point their abdomens skywards and cast long lines of silk into the breeze. As the wind catches the lengthening threads the arachnids are lifted into the air to sail away to pastures new, the fallen silk creating the beautiful, ephemeral mantle I see before me. Such a dispersal mechanism, known as 'ballooning', would be incredible enough in itself but this phenomenon seems also to involve the spider being able to detect the slightest change in atmospheric electrical fields using hair-like sensors on each of its eight legs. Along with wind speed, additional forces for lift-off are provided via the negatively charged silk thread that repels the charge of the grasses they are perched upon to launch the spiders from their earthbound platform. A grassland free from pesticides is one filled with hidden life.

26th November

One tree species above all others stands out in late autumn and it is not one that you would expect to see in the Northamptonshire countryside. Towering above the mature canopies of earthy alders that fringe the riverside close to my summer swimming spot, a cluster of five dawn redwoods, their flattened feathery needles unremarkable for much of the year, have collectively burst into flaming pyramidal spires soaring against a backdrop of a flat-calm river and dormant water meadows. Though conifers are often evergreen, the dawn redwood sheds its leaves by winter and beneath broad, buttressed bases of fissured trunks, toasted saffron coloured needles are liberally sprinkled amongst the damp soils and yellowing sedges. I pick up a fallen branch, strip off a handful of needles, and catch the faintest whiff of resinous perfume.

The low sun is beginning to catch subtle undulations in the meadow beyond, picking out strips of pale-green peaks above shallow furrows cast in shadow. In the cold still air a pair of jackdaws escort a sparrowhawk out of their territory. Large flocks of clinking goldfinches are busy in the alders, zealously searching out the abundant seed held within small disarticulating cones. Every so often they peel away in a loose cloud but soon circle back to the high canopy, like tumbling leaves drawn back to the branches. Fieldfares chatter in the distance. All these sights and sounds are alien to the redwoods' native homeland. These trees have a story to tell before winter once again blends them into the background.

They appear to have been rooted to the spot for centuries, overlooked on the rise of the hill by their giant redwood cousins that were planted in Victorian times. In fact, the dawn redwoods can only have been here for around sixty or seventy years, which makes their height and girth all the more remarkable. They belong to the genus Metasequoia, the most dominant tree on Earth 100 million years ago, sharing the land with the dominant fauna, dinosaurs. Catastrophic events that wiped out the giant lizards/chickens appeared to have also sealed the fate of the trees, with palaeobotanists dating the dawn redwood's extinction to about five million years ago, give or take a few millennia. But in the 1940s a Chinese forester, Gan Duo, working in a remote and mountainous landscape close to the Sichuan-Hubei border, discovered a tree that he could not immediately identify. Word soon spread to Professor Cheng of the National Central University in China and in 1946 Cheng led an expedition to this remote outpost to collect specimens for study. Working with the country's leading dendrologist, it soon became apparent that Gan Duo had discovered a 'living fossil', an ancient tree from the 'dawn' of time. Hence the name, dawn redwood.

The botanical discovery of the century did not go unnoticed, and in the following year seeds reached the Director of the Arnold Arboretum of Harvard University in Boston, who then distributed them amongst botanic gardens in the United States and Europe for cultivation. And soon after, somehow, five saplings found their way to our rural village in the middle of England and were planted out in damp soil by someone who clearly was both well connected and knew what they were doing, as this is precisely the type of ground that the tree prefers. There are now over a million dawn redwoods planted across the globe, originally deriving from the seeds of just a handful of trees, and all thanks to an inquisitive forester who took the time to pause and look more closely at the world around him.

2nd December

By late afternoon when the sun is just a pinch above the horizon, resident starlings, together with large numbers of wintering migrants, fill the threadbare architecture of mature ash, oak and sycamore, noisily congregate in fields of winter wheat, flock to meeting points within ancient meadows and pasture, gather together along hedgerows and woodland margins, on telephone wires and slate roofs.

Assembled at the final staging post of their daily commute, as the light fades to a seemingly very specific frequency, these disparate bands of gregarious birds launch into the air as a living wind. They barrel along at waist height in tight fluid formations, hugging the ground, brushing the tops of crops and faded grasses, effortlessly rising without missing a beat to skim over hedges and treetops, houses and stone walls, then fall to follow an invisible contour that dips under the predator's radar. They are all speeding to the same destination, the same place I am pedalling hard towards.

Standing by the river, next to a hedge cloaked in bramble, I scan the western horizon, looking out over the largest gravel pit, catching my breath. The last sliver of sun begins to disappear beyond a herd of cattle grazing close to reed-fringed margins, high clouds turning shades of rose pink, burnished orange and gold, their colours reflected on the expanse of water, blending with blues and blacks and greens. A large group of starlings is gathering in the tilled brown fields that border the gravel pits, perched snugly together on electricity cables, thickening sections of lines where they congregate. As more arrive some birds spill down to the ground whilst others rise up to fill the gaps left behind. My focus is on this arable field in the distance when a huge flock in tight formation suddenly pour in over my right shoulder, the rushing sound of countless beating wings coursing between a gap in the hedge only a couple of metres away from where I stand, open-mouthed. I start to count as the sinuous line of birds floods the pasture ahead, skimming over the cattle fence, snaking towards the reeds and then up towards mature willows and the arable field beyond. After fifteen seconds the solid flow of starlings is still streaming past.

To the soundtrack of whistling wildfowl and honking greylag geese sharing the grazing grounds, the collective stationed in the arable field rises to meet with these fresh arrivals and the standout performance of the winter months begins.

Distant specks of countless numbers of starlings are strung out in an undulating line perhaps a kilometre or more across. A few seconds later they bunch together and come sweeping over the pits and grassland, then separate into multiple granular shapes, each concentrated mass containing many thousands of birds and regularly supplemented by smaller squadrons late to the party, dashing in from the surrounding landscape, linking seamlessly to the whole. One mass fly ever closer until the birds are coursing overhead, gliding in silent synchrony. I look up to see a flowing jigsaw of black, star-shaped cut-outs against a purple background, each bird maintaining precisely the same distance from its neighbours, a perfect pattern repeated over and over and over again, wings stiff and outstretched, the sky filled with countless identical forms. Then the noise of their beating wings, like a breaking wave on a shingle beach as they turn as one, drift high over the reeds and then suddenly fracture into black and grey amorphous blobs, the sky a giant lava lamp of pulsing forms. I spot whales, anvils, planets, twisting hourglass figures and tornadoes sweeping across the horizon, ellipses constantly shape-shifting, their densities splitting, expanding, compressing, dissipating, reforming. Then dense black surges, accelerating waves created by sudden changes of direction, speed through one of the larger flocks, the form appearing to pivot on its axis.

The creation of such spectacular, hypnotic patterns is breathtaking, but this performance is not for my benefit. It represents an agitated flock responding dynamically to a perceived threat. The birds are right to be nervous as, seconds later, the sleek silhouette of a sparrowhawk comes speeding into view, puncturing one of the organic shapes and causing in a split second the whole to burst apart into two giant spheres. The reaction time of the starlings is properly impressive but the predator's actions have the desired effect, isolating a few birds from the safety of the pack, these vulnerable starlings fleeing for their lives, the tawny hawk in pursuit, driving them down with powerful beats of its broad stiff wings, chasing them low over the water, bright white bib flashing, angle of attack constantly adjusting, until prey and predator disappear from my sight behind willow scrub. It looks bad for the starlings, but the hawk will be unsuccessful about nine times out of ten.

Mesmeric, rhythmic aerial displays continue for close to half an hour, by which time I have circled around to where the starlings are beginning to roost. With each pass, drifting globular formations morph into funnel shapes, releasing narrow columns of birds at the tip that pour into the relative safety of a bronzed curtain of reeds. Occasionally an entire group rains down, but more often than not the bulk of the flock lurches upwards at the last moment, perhaps spooked by another waiting hawk. As time passes and numbers gradually thin out to the last nervous hundred or so, darkness begins to fall. The starlings rapidly turn and twist together, each waiting for the other to make the first move, sweeping just a few metres above the feathered reeds until finally, inevitably, they drop and the sky is empty, save for a few late arrivals, singletons skimming over the fields and diving straight in.

Their exhilarating murmuration at an end, a cacophonous noise starts up, breaking my trance as the thousands of starlings that so recently filled the sky now jostle for space backstage in a packed reedbed, tussling for prime locations to bed down for the night. The light has almost gone. Numb toes alert me to a drop in temperature not previously realised. Hands placed firmly in coat pockets, I turn for home, pausing briefly to silently acknowledge my good fortune to live within walking distance of such an astonishing, uplifting performance.

6th December

Following a narrow lane, past a steaming heap of dung and straw piled high in a field corner, fresh from the barns where cows are bedding down for the winter months, I reach the arable field overlooking the gravel pits and reedbeds. The light is fading and I am eager to witness a repeat of the murmuration. But rather than forming spectacular shapes, the starlings instead stream past in a long flowing line straight into the reeds, without hesitation. The whole event is over before it has begun. I wait for a while, just in case a second wave arrives, but it is fairly clear that there will be no show tonight. Whilst it is good to be reminded from time to time that every sighting is unique, and I'll take the thrill of chance happenings over predictable events any day, it is slightly disappointing nonetheless. As I cross the wooden bridge that leads out of the reserve, a rapid high-pitched peeping noise is followed by a flashing bullet of vibrant blue and orange. A kingfisher banks sharply to trace the centre of the channel, its compact body whirring over the water, perfectly visible for a few seconds before vanishing with the curve of the brook. I smile to myself, lesson learnt.

10th December

As autumn faces winter, most trees and shrubs have long since lost their modesty but thick mature oaks flanking the lanes and covering chunks of woodland continue to cling on to their crinkled golden-brown leaves, some still mottled with a stubborn green. Most if not all of these leaves will eventually be torn off by strong winds or fall with heavy snow as the season beds in, but just now you can spot an oak from a mile away.

The phenomenon of delayed leaf fall is called marcescence, literally meaning 'to wither'. Leaves have at the base of their stalks a layer of cells that cement them to the twig. As photosynthesis ends and sugars stop being made, these cells start to weaken so that, eventually, the leaf has little or nothing securing it to its anchor. This weakened point at the tip of the stalk is known as the abscission layer. But in some species, such as our oaks, this layer is incomplete, meaning that although the leaf's food supply is cut, it remains intact. You might imagine that we would know why some trees retain their leaves in winter whilst others do not, but in fact while a name has been put to this phenomenon, the ecological advantages afforded by marcescence are still mostly speculative. Perhaps the most plausible explanation put forward suggests that leaves hanging on until the spring act as a fertiliser for the soil as they fall, just when awakening trees are better able to use it. But it's really just a best guess and I'm not convinced that it would stand up to closer scrutiny.

It would appear that the elms, at least in our area, are similarly reluctant to relinquish their jagged-edged foliage to the waiting worms, bacteria and fungal hordes below, and now is the perfect time to appreciate just what an important component this species remains along the kilometres of hedgerow that criss-cross our parish. Whilst almost all of our mature elm trees are long gone, these once magnificent specimens first dealt a slow death by microscopic fungal spores transported by tiny bark beetles and then finished off by chainsaws, their roots are usually not killed. And like blackthorn, another ever-present of hedges here, elms are more than capable of growing horizontally, as well as vertically. This form of growth has preserved the elm as a micro-version of its former self, although there is a price to pay for outfoxing the disease. Shoots will never survive to reach the heights of their forebears, always destined to hide amongst the thorns, for if they rise more than five metres above the ground their presence to the bark beetle is signalled, and their fate sealed.

15th December

Venturing outside when the weather consists entirely of cold, steady rain is not a happy proposition. Such days are made for embracing the warmth and comfort of home, though the dog seems not to share this widely held opinion. Fortunately, it is not always raining. Clear, still skies overnight have combined with freezing temperatures to create a dramatically altered and uplifting landscape.

From a distance, it looks as though the land running down to the river is shrouded in a fine dusting of icing sugar. Blades of grass, cushions of sparkling moss and drifts of fallen leaves, their margins thick with frost, crunch underfoot. Small puddles encased under thin, clear ice shatter with the lightest touch. Paths and trackways that only yesterday were a slippery mudfest are now as hard as iron, the recent imprints and skids of walkers, vehicles and animals set fast in temporary moulds. Fencelines surrounding meadows and pastures are masked in tightly packed ice crystals that curve to follow twists of barbed wire. Where sheep have snagged against sharp knots, icy wool dangles like long strings of stiff linguine.

A closer look at entwined brambles and roses, hanging branches, metal gates and fenceposts reveals the densest arrangement of ice crystals on surfaces most exposed to the elements. These crystals are elongated and finely pointed, stitched together into delicate feathering patterns, thickening and exaggerating the faces on which they have assembled. This exquisite phenomenon coating the landscape is known as a hoar frost, which happens when cold water vapour in the air comes into contact with surfaces that are already below freezing point. Ice crystals form instantly and continue to grow in fractal patterns as more water vapour accumulates.[20]

The early winter scene is at its most picturesque in the sole water meadow that is not grazed or cut but left to its own devices, where the slender, arching stems of tufted hair-grass mix with broad-leaved sedges and tall robust frames of hogweed and angelica, their outlines accentuated by needle-fringed crystalline borders. I walk up to take a photo of one particularly striking plant and accidentally flush a couple of snipe hidden in the dense vegetation. Taken aback by their sudden emergence, I take a sharp intake of freezing air as they shoot into the sky in a rapid, jinking flight. The waders circle high overhead, dark specks against a washed-out pale blue, looking down on an exhaling river and a landscape in a state of suspended animation.

---

[20] The rather odd prefix 'hoar' derives from the Old English for 'old' or 'venerable' and is an oblique reference to the 'beards' of ice that form along the edges of otherwise bare twigs and branches.

The frost has created a perfect winter scene, but standing to admire it does not warm the bones and after a while the intense cold starts to seep through my layers. I head back home, past the freshly picked carcass of a cock pheasant, and imagine foxes full and warm in their earth.

The Cuckoo (Part V)

Daydreaming of warmer times, my thoughts turn briefly to the cuckoo, long departed and currently living out its days in central Africa within a patchwork of grassland, near-impenetrable swamp and tropical forest. They will be feasting on large juicy caterpillars that would have transformed into moths given half a chance, sharing their surroundings with chimpanzees, serpent eagles, antelopes, cheetahs. It all seems so impossibly distant.

21st December

It is the winter solstice, "the still point of the sun... where the past lets go of and becomes the future", as Margaret Atwood so memorably framed it.[21]

As plants go, hemlock (*Conium maculatum*) is not considered worthy of much fanfare, dismissed as a common species that persists in grotty, neglected land. To some extent that is a fair summation and its association with folklore does not help matters, being implicated in the poisoning of Socrates,[22] although the source of the Athenian's downfall is more likely to have been hemlock water-dropwort (*Oenanthe crocata*) – similar common

---

[21] *Shapechangers In Winter*
[22] The philosopher, not the elegant Brazilian footballer of the 1980s

name, very different species. Given a choice between seeing hemlock or a fancy orchid, it would be no contest for most, like comparing the aesthetic thrill of a multi-storey car park with a grade II listed Cotswold cottage. But whilst the orchid is reduced to a rosette of leaves held flat to the turf in the winter months, or has disappeared entirely underground, the skeletal frames of hemlock endure as proud 2.5m stands of brutalist architectural complexity, lending structure to the landscape alongside teasels and hogweed, providing perches and food for goldfinch, siskin and redpoll.

Growing in unkempt grassland by the river, backlit by a pale-orange solstice sun, mist rising from the blue-grey river, the shortest days are its time to shine.

23rd December

Rain falls out of a clear blue sky as the temperature rises with the sun to melt ice-encrusted branches.

A few years ago, following a short dash to catch a train that took most of the two-hour journey to recover from, I decided to take up jogging after a lifetime of abstinence. Indeed, I was so late to the starting line that even the verb for this activity had changed, 'to jog' being replaced at some point by 'to run', which I can't help thinking is a cunning marketing ploy that allows us to believe we could all be elite athletes if we only bought the correct shoes and neon lycra.

To my great surprise, I eventually found plodding (no lycra for me) to be enjoyable, especially when the activity is offset by the sight of wildlife that shares my route. In the winter months, and depending on which route I take, fieldfares and redwings, starlings, red kites, wigeon and teal are reliable company, along with flocks of goldfinch, long-tailed tits and the usual hedgerow suspects such as dunnock, blue tit, greenfinch, blackbird and robin. Egrets, both little and great, usually make themselves known at some point if I am gulping for air by the gravel pits, as do stately grey herons. Cormorants can often be seen perching by the waterside, wings outstretched, not waving but drying.[23] I prefer not to cut off the soundscape by plugging into a podcast or playlist. Fleeting snatches of birdsong can reveal hidden gems, as well as providing an excellent excuse to catch my breath. This afternoon, as the sun stretches my shadow, a burst of shrill, high-pitched notes draws my gaze up to the top of a straggly hawthorn and two tiny, plump profiles.

The goldcrest is one of the smallest birds in the northern hemisphere, weighing about five grammes, roughly the heft of a 20p piece. Their tubby appearance is accentuated by a relatively large head, the lack of any neck to speak of, and a short bill and tail. A rather dull olive-green colouration is more than made up for by a striking yellow flame licking the top of the head, bordered in black, sometimes raised by the male like a mohican in an effort to attract a mate during the breeding season, or when it is feeling particularly aggrieved. They have a restless, lively nature and body-pop through tree tops, their beaks manically cleaning insects the size of punctuation marks from branches, dislodging tiny eggs hidden in the fissures of bark or in the clefts of mosses, lichens and ivy that cling to trunks and twigs.

---

[23] With apologies to Stevie Smith

For such a small bird they have a rather grand mythology. The story goes that there was once a contest to determine the 'King of the Birds', won by the contestant that could fly highest. The eagle, with more than a hint of arrogance, assumed that he had the title in the bag as he soared above, leaving all others behind. Or so he thought. For as he began to tire, a tiny goldcrest that had hidden in the eagle's tail feathers popped out and flew above the spent bird, claiming the crown from the sun. The memory of this fable lives on in the Latin binomial for the goldcrest, *Regulus regulus*, or 'Little king'. And you can add strength to their cunning as incredibly, for such a light bird, every autumn hundreds of thousands of goldcrests migrate from Scandinavia to our eastern shores. In the past some birds would rest on the rigging of trawlers out in the North Sea, giving rise to another nickname, the 'herring spink', although the birds would struggle to find a herring trawler these days. And in a nice echo of the original fable, there remained for some time a suspicion that the goldcrest was simply too small to undertake such a journey, so must have hidden in the plumage of owls or woodcock that accompanied them on their migration route.

28th December

There is a reason why the fields that cover the valley floor are known as flood meadows. After 24 hours of biblical rainfall, the low-lying land has been consumed by the river. A bitter northerly wind spirals kites high above a landscape suddenly transformed. Viewed from the highest point in the village where giant redwoods stand as sentinels, marooned lines of telegraph poles rise like the masts of sunken ships. In the vast waterscape, fractions of hedgerow sporadically break the surface and grass outcrops are exposed as green fingered islands, a magnet for roaming geese. Where not so long ago there were cattle grazing, swans now glide, wildfowl sing out and black-headed gulls wheel above as busy white specks.

It is impossible to know how deep the water lies over the grassland, but the new reflective skin envelops square kilometres and levels will continue to rise for a while yet, the delayed effect of rain falling on tiles, roads, patios and driveways further upstream where towns have crept ever closer to the river. Landing on impermeable soils, the excess waters gravitate to meet with the main artery, disappearing downstream with expensive engineering, out of sight and out of mind, congregating and swelling to breach our banks, settling over fields rather than forecourts, living rooms and kitchens. Instead of reaping destruction, here the annual floods bring life and fertility, sediments churned up from the riverbed brought inland and deposited, adding nutrients to feed the soil and in time the vegetation, the livestock, and us. Most of the plants that grow in water meadows are adapted to such conditions, and indeed many depend on periodic flooding to thrive and disperse.

As the river continues to rise to find its level, a minor road that bisects the oxbow and connects our village to the next becomes submerged, cutting us off from the main road beyond. Standing on the bridge nearest to home, about forty metres before the road disappears, and peering over the edge, the raw power of the river in spate is an awesome sight and sound. Close to one metric tonne of water per second roars through its archways. It seems incredible that this structure can withstand such a prodigious, continuous surge of sandy-brown water swelling and heaving against angled stone buttresses that have been rooted to the river bed for five centuries. The three-metre gap between the river and the top of each arch during the summer is now reduced to thirty centimetres as the thunderous torrent squeezes through, creating swirling vortices that dance downstream. But once past this pinch point there is space for the river to spread out, its energy gradually dissipating as it relaxes over the meadows.

When the road becomes impassable, folk are forewarned by a hinged iron road sign which is covered for much of the year by a blank plate but now reveals clear advice in rusting white lettering against a bright red peeling background – FLOODS. Though tempting, it is usually not possible, or advisable, to try to wade on through with wellies. Quite apart from the fact that the flow can be deceptively fast, even in seemingly shallow water, and could easily sweep a sturdy soul off their feet, the road is uneven with hidden dips lying in wait like bear traps. Most drivers who ignore the warning sign stop as they reach the water's edge, pause to fight the urge of forward momentum and invincibility and then turn around to find an alternative route.

But for some, and it seems especially those with shiny 4x4 vehicles, overconfidence mixed with perhaps a touch of indignation is quickly overtaken by spluttering, stalling hubris and a very expensive phone call.

1st January

The winter floodwaters have lifted a large stone, far too heavy for a human to budge. Its new placement subtly changes the water's flow, causing a diversion that creates rippling patterns where previously there were none.

5th January

In medieval times the red kite was a familiar sight across lowland England, tolerated for performing an essential service, scavenging for scraps of discarded food in towns and villages. But memories soon fade, attitudes and perceptions change and by the 1600s, as its numbers grew, the kite was viewed not as a necessary waste-disposal unit but as unwanted vermin, stealing food and spreading disease. Such misinformation and vilification continued and as kite numbers fell due to persecution, tall tales of its thievery and cunning escalated, coinciding with the increasingly popular pastime (by those who had the means) of shooting pheasants and partridges.

It was said that gamebirds and even lambs were being taken, although the kite weighs only a kilo and survives almost entirely on carrion, rodents, beetles, worms and invertebrates. By the end of the 19th century this magnificent bird of prey had been poisoned and shot to extinction in England.

In 1995, almost one hundred years after the last kite had been rubbed out from our landscape, eleven birds of Spanish descent were released into the wild, some in the adjacent parish barely 1 km west from here. This was to be the beginnings of the most successful reintroduction project undertaken in these Isles, but when we moved to Northamptonshire the kite was still a rare and exciting sight, worthy of slamming on the brakes, pulling over into the nearest layby, fumbling for binoculars in the glove compartment in the hope of getting a better view. Fast-forward twenty years and they are now as common a sound in the skies above the village as jackdaws. It is not at all uncommon to see four or five kites circling the thermals at any given time, to hear their high-pitched mewing on a stroll to the local store. Friends who come to stay will let out the occasional expletive as the raptors bank to swoop low over our garden, their broad, deeply forked cinnamon rudders turning to steer and sail the birds only a few metres above their heads, showing off impressive two-metre wingspans displaying a beautiful mix of rufous, white and black-tipped plumage.

Inevitably, the excitement of seeing something for the first time gradually fades with familiarity. It can be curiously easy to become flippant about living in close proximity to such a majestic creature, taken for granted like the mature oaks and limes or the masterfully constructed stone walls that wrap around the village. They become a part of the whole, which is not necessarily a bad thing, as history tells us what happens when the kite becomes too successful, too quickly. In recent years I've begun to hear and read echoes of the past. The kite has been labelled as a 'pest' in some newspaper articles, a danger to us all as they snatch sausage rolls from the hands of unwary children, carry off our free-range chickens and pet cats. One person who I had thought to be moderately level-headed voiced the fear that soon kites would be breeding with buzzards, creating some kind of chimera super-predator, presumably. Still, I like to think such tall tales, ignorance and urban myths are for the minority and that most feel a sense of repentant pride at reinstating this wonderful bird to share the skies with buzzards and ravens, two other persecuted birds driven to the margins of existence in the past, but now repopulating lowland woods and fields, free to do so without being shot or poisoned to oblivion. Well, not legally, anyway.

With a flourishing population so close to home, it is possible to learn more about them and to witness some spectacular behaviour, without really having to try too hard. This morning an adult bird was perched on a thick branch jutting out from a nearby ash and through my telescope, set up in the warmth of my office, I was able to study its curved beak, yellow nearest the eyes but fading to dark grey and then black at the razor-sharp business end. The eyes themselves are encircled by a yellow ring, setting off a striking watery-grey iris, sometimes appearing almost white, and deep black pupils. In the spring I've seen entangled birds tumbling from the sky, two rivals with talons locked in mid-air cartwheeling towards the ground, only separating at the last moment as the earth rises to meet them. A few years ago, I found the location of their main winter roost, where sometimes upwards of 100 kites circle in a darkening sky. It is an awesome sight. I cannot imagine this place without them.

9th January

Backlit by the rising sun, a barn owl patrols wide margins spared from the plough. These perimeters are the perfect environment for a supermarket of small rodents to flourish amongst tussocky grasses and brambles that stray into wild hedgerows. Such boundaries on arable land are often unproductive, the yield either eaten away by flocks of pigeons or the ground too wet or too shaded to achieve a respectable return. These wild, uncropped fragments soon add up when multiplied across the local landscape, giving colour and life to the margins as well as aiding the pollination of crops.

Hunger has most likely drawn this owl out into the morning light. Unlike the waterfowl calling from flooded meadows below, barn owls produce no oil to preen with, and instead of straight edges creating turbulence and amplifying the sound of beating wings, each of the owl's soft feathers has a curved edge to stabilise and streamline airflow. This deadens sound through a combination of comb-like serrations on the leading edge and a soft fringe on the trailing edge. But there is a cost to this evolutionary advantage. It has been steadily raining for the past few days and its feathers are easily waterlogged. Without the means of flight, their ability to hunt is lost. Fortunately for the owl this morning has, at last, brought with it clear skies.

Silent flight not only helps to make the owl inaudible to its prey, it also ensures that it can hear skittering footsteps, for though barn owls have exceptional vision, victims are usually located not by sight, but by sound. Its heart-shaped face acts like a radar dish and contains facial muscles that guide the slightest noise towards hidden ears positioned just behind the eyes, one sitting higher than the other. In this way, the owl can detect and calculate precisely the position of prey concealed in dense undergrowth.

In flight the barn owl looks almost comically disproportioned, its white lightweight bobbing body trying to keep up with steady beats of its broad, oversized buff-coloured wings, spanning close to a metre. But these too help inaudible flight, as little flapping is required. The owl reaches a likely spot for breakfast and begins to gracefully glide, swoop and turn, quartering the ground. I stand amazed at my luck, knowing that at any moment the owl could simply drift over a hedge and be lost from my sight. Sharing space with a barn owl feels like a privilege, though the voles probably don't share my reverence as death stalks them on silent wings.

The owl drifts to haunt the untidy space between young barley and a thorn hedge, then stops abruptly only a hundred metres or so from where I am standing, transfixed. Blurred muted wings apply the brakes to hang a few metres above rank grasses, its head turned, dipped towards the earth, pinpointing a faint high-frequency squeak. Locked-on, in a split-second rounded wing-tips point to the sky, legs and talons extend and the ghost drops like a dagger to disappear from view.

14th January

The flood waters have subsided and the river has resumed its familiar form, reflective depressions in the fields the only sign that the whole area once resembled an inland sea. Solid paths scrunch underfoot, a welcome respite from the mud baths created by rainfall and regular human traffic. As the sun rises, the frost-covered surfaces of grassland and hedgerows, of metal gates, fallen leaves and plump molehills sparkle with constantly shifting specks of light, as if a glitter bomb had been detonated overnight.

Down by the water meadows a great white egret flies languidly by, coasting over tufts of rushes sticking up like unruly cowlicks. A linnet perched on an orange crack willow twig sings out its sweet melody before diving down to become hidden within stiff frosted grasses. A pale half-moon hangs around while tinkling goldfinches feed on the seed heads of teasel and burdock, the latter's prickly burs laden with miniature fish hooks perfectly adapted for dispersal on the feet and fur of the dog. Every so often the tops of fence posts have a scattering of discarded pale-yellow rose hip seeds, perhaps the remains of a snack by a migrant thrush, evidence of the seeds' ability to survive the digestive process. By mid morning the ground frost has withdrawn to the shadows, lingering in sheltered corners while sun-struck surfaces gradually reveal an austere landscape of faded greens, dark purples and browns, all settled under a vast and brilliant blue.

18th January

It is another cold and atmospheric start to the day, with
freezing temperatures overnight stubbornly persisting as
the sun labours to break through a dense white haze. As
I leave the house the cracking staccato sound of gunfire,
very different from the muffled flump of a gas gun
scattering pigeons, echoes across the water meadows. It
does not take a genius to walk in the opposite direction.

Sitting as a sinuous island between arable land rolling
down to meet its northern rushy margins, a popular
trout fishery to the west and the willow-lined gravel pits
to the south and east, a pocket-sized but pristine area of
ancient fen vegetation[24] somehow remained intact as all
around carnage ensued. Seventy years ago, huge craters
that would in time be left to fill with water and wildfowl
began to gradually take shape as aggregates were worked
out. How the fen didn't suffer the same fate as the
surrounding fields is lost with the memories of those
who made the decisions about where to dig, for there
are certainly gravels underneath its surface, judging by
the vegetation and trickling runnels that percolate and
meander down to meet the boundary brook.

Almost as soon as I'm over the cattle gate and into
the fen, three elusive jack snipe, winter visitors from
far-flung corners of northern Europe and impossible
to spot unless flushed, burst from a wide belt of frozen
blunt-flowered rush. Their diminutive, straight-beaked
dark forms shoot off in an unswerving shallow line to
be lost in a hanging mist that keeps visibility to only

---

[24] A type of species-rich wetland vegetation fed by mineral-rich ground
water

100m or so. I imagine the indiscernible landscape beyond as it might have been 100 years ago, with larger areas of fen dotted around rich expanses of grassland, but my daydream is soon broken by the whistling calls of teal and wigeon, sounds that could only arrive after the turf, soil and gravels had been lost.

The ground, frozen solid on the walk down, here remains soft underfoot, seepages saturated where water continues to rise and collect. In the spring and summer months, chiffchaffs and other warblers will sing out from the nearby canopy of a large wandering willow filling out a circular depression. This place will be alive with insect life. It will be bright with kingcups, marsh valerian, cuckooflower, willowherbs, marsh orchids, statuesque marsh thistles. If you know where to search, one or two frilly white flowers of bogbean might be found at this its only surviving site in the county. Just now, though, the fen lies dormant under a white frosting. Tussock sedges like miniature haystacks have formed colonies on marginally higher ground, their leaves and long inflorescences munched down to neat cropped hummocks by cattle now warm in their shed.

As I walk on towards the fen's eastern edge two more snipe, perfectly camouflaged in the rusting rushes, bolt from beneath my feet and rocket into the mist. It is easy to see why they are sometimes called 'heart-attack' birds. It is impossible to know how many more lie hunkered down, keenly aware of my presence, primed and ready to cause more palpitations if I wander too close. Deciding not to try to find out, I move up to where the fenceline meets bare arable soils. Frost crystals trace the circular grain of wooden fenceposts. Two wrens with cocked tails flit amongst bramble and barbed wire, so close I can see their cream eye stripes and a white speckled patterning on rich-brown wings.

Near to the brook a mature white willow has, in the past, split in two. One section remains upright, old and gnarly, but the other wanders along the ground from its central breaking point, long ago becoming intertwined with soil and sedges, dipping and weaving under and over its neighbours. The fissured bark of the fallen trunk, resembling a lurking crocodile, is softened by spreading pleurocarpous mosses, encrusted with splodges of green, grey and yellow lichens. A few sections have lost their protective outer layer, the exposed wood now pliable, easily broken up and crumbled between my fingers. Some areas are punctured with tiny boreholes where insects have set up residence. A solid horseshoe-shaped fungal bracket, rust brown above and a pure white beneath, juts out from the base of the break, cream-coloured mycelium exposed between the bark. This recumbent willow stem is, however, far from dead. The catastrophic event that resulted in its downfall fractured but did not completely sever it from the surviving upright bole, and over time it has sprouted new adventitious roots that lie anchored deep within the soil. When once there was a single crown, the reborn tree now holds eight thick vertical limbs rising at crooked angles, their heights ranging from four or five to over ten metres tall, together forming a long sinuous hedge-like sculpture rising from damp, fertile earth.

The sun is starting to burn its way through the mist, an opaque sphere fading in and out through a veil of a billion droplets, until gradually the temperature climbs above freezing point and the balance begins to shift. Light escaping from the mist reveals details previously hidden in dark silhouettes, and a white sky gently transitions to blue, until the fen is washed in a sparkling burnished gold.

25th January

I haven't been up to the woodland since November, its allure tempered by rutted muddy paths and slopes. It is quite hard going when every step slides you sideways. Even when the clay soil is baked dry in the summer months it takes at least half a day to get to and from the woods and properly appreciate the walk and wildlife. But after days of mizzling rain, today the sky is clear, two main chunks of work are finished and much of the way is firm, or firm enough, due to an overnight ground frost.

My wellingtons crack icy veneers into angled shards as I deliberately press on puddles that fill potholes along the green lane, taking pleasure in the patterns that form instantly. Along with a flock of wandering long-tailed tits and fieldfares, by now a familiar sight, a pair of bullfinches keep me company, their black caps, like mine, pulled tight over their heads.

The final kilometre up to the woodland, along the margin of a large arable field, has been churned up by what must have been quite a sizable herd of deer. The prints resemble those of fallow, the indentations having two slightly pointed toes and a rounded heel. Roe deer, much the less common of the two species here, have tracks that are widely spaced and splay outwards.[25] They

---

[25] Resembling Star Trek's Mr Spock's 'Live long and prosper' hand gesture

are definitely not signs of muntjac, a much smaller deer that doesn't yet roam the lowlands in large packs. The tracks lead to and from the direction of the wood, and the route I walk is clearly a main thoroughfare for the deer. It is pleasing to follow the prints and imagine how the scene might change as the light fades and a steady stream of large mammals flows through this landscape.

Lichen-encrusted blackthorn and oak line the edges and entrance to the wood, their branches adorned with flakes of mint-green, yellow, orange and gold. It is easy to imagine the relief the deer might experience as they pass through this portal, back into the safety of dense undergrowth and tall canopies filtering light, casting shade, leaving the exposed farmed plains behind. The high-pitched melody of blackbirds, deep hollow croaks of ravens and loud thrum and purr of a quad bike greet me when I enter the wood, the bike's handler methodically navigating his way around fallen branches, his black labrador running alongside. It is unusual to see anyone here, let alone man, machine and dog, and their presence scatters two flighty muntjac that run and leap towards and past me, letting out a noise somewhere between a bark and a guttural belch as they disappear from view. It is not the most tranquil scene to begin a woodland walk, but the noise of the bike soon diminishes, leaving an exaggerated stillness trailing in its wake.

The sharp delineation between ancient woodland and conifer plantation is now at its most obvious. Leaves of the former litter the forest floor, dark chocolate and molasses colours blending with muscovado, chestnut and caramel, all in various states of slow decomposition. The dead leaves nestle next to healthy mosses, plumped up and pristine-looking, ripe for identification after spending the spring and summer in desiccated anonymity. After several brief attempts over the years, I am pleased to find that I can still drag a few species' names from the depths of my memory bank. Common tamarisk-moss *Thuidium tamariscinum*, a stunning yellow-green species resembling a micro-fern, and a nice indicator of quality woodland, sits in layered clumps next to patches of common feather-moss *Kindbergia praelonga* and the beautiful translucent leaves of hart's-tongue thyme-moss *Plagiomnium undulatum*. Scores of other mosses that I have yet to learn, or have learnt and forgotten and must at some point learn again, line leaning trunks with rough bark made velvet soft. They creep up the foundations of thick contorted stumps, tumble among the bases of winter-green sedges and the straw-coloured remains of tufted grasses. Most passers-by will take for granted the myriad of seemingly similar species, all growing together, but it is worth taking the time to pause and examine these primitive plants, ideally using a hand lens, in much the same way you would when using a pair of binoculars for an improved view of birdlife. Simply taking a moment to examine their beautifully intricate structures and colours, and the life that lives within them, is enough to be temporarily transported into worlds within worlds.

Contrasting with the ancient broadleaved is the modern coniferous woodland, dark-green needles of spruce and pine persisting in evergreen canopies, the floor beneath dry and relatively bare. At a distance the plantation appears as a dark, impenetrable void, contrasting with the diverse and welcoming tones the ancient has to offer. There is, however, an aesthetic beauty to the regimented rows of softwood trunks when their faces are illuminated by a low sun casting evenly spaced shadows across a sunlit floor. I walk a few paces and view the trees from a different angle, with the sun directly behind the conifers, admiring a sea of thin silhouettes enveloped in an auburn haze.

Heading deeper into the wood, binoculars poised, a small brown shape not much bigger than a wren attracts my attention scuttling up and around the trunk of an oak; it's a treecreeper, or as I knew it as a teenager growing up in the south-west, a tree-mouse. The bird explores crevices for insects and spiders with a long, downcurved beak, its mottled brown and black plumage blending with the bark it is investigating, the camouflaged bird only given away by a staccato hopping motion (a bit like a mouse) as it spirals upwards. A buzzard briefly comes into view, gliding low over the bare treetops, a hulking giant in comparison. It comes to rest for a moment almost directly above me and the treecreeper, the light-brown and white plumage on its belly just visible through a maze of branches.

The treecreeper is a fairly sedentary bird, preferring to stay within a small territory, happy with its lot. Much like a woodpecker, it uses its long stiff tail to push against the trunk of a tree to provide support and grips with sharp, arched claws. But whilst it is a master at creeping up or across a tree, due to the fixed shape of its toes it is incapable of climbing down. So, when the bird reaches the summit, it has no choice but to drift down to the base of the same tree, or the one adjacent, to begin again its ascent. Not the end of the world, really, for a creature that has the power of flight.

After leaving the treecreeper to its steady work and following a narrow ride for a while, I find myself approaching the familiar hardstanding forestry track cutting through the centre of the wood. This comes as a bit of surprise, as I thought I was heading in precisely the opposite direction. A sense of direction is not one of my strong points, as many family members and colleagues can testify. Emerging into the open, I disturb a flock of redwings turning over leaves and small chunks of bark in search of food. They scatter into the crown of a nearby ash, then move on down the track, singing as they go. Remembering that I have an unopened flask of coffee in my rucksack, and as home is now further away than expected, I decide to take a break by the side of the track.

As I'm inwardly praising myself for having the foresight to pack a hot drink, seven fallow does casually wander out of the wood and into view, almost opposite to where I am sitting. I watch them feeding, their heads bent to munch grassy margins, the coffee held in my hand slowly releasing its warmth to the cold air. Inevitably, one doe soon catches my scent, or the smell of the coffee, it's hard to tell, but not before I've had time to study a twitching black tail masking a bright-white rump and a speckled winter coat bathed in the dipping sun, grading in colour from dark brown to fawn to a golden-tan. Her head snaps up, long ears pricked, body perfectly still, focus absolute. A binary decision is reached, instinct kicks in and she twists her substantial form to crash away through brambles, her companions fleeing in synchrony, heavy legs hammering into the hidden depths of leggy hazel coppice.

I take a sip of my now lukewarm beverage and pick up a ride at right angles to the main track that leads down to the margin I followed up to the wood earlier in the day, cloven imprints no longer just abstract markings in the soil. Giant shadows of boundary oaks roam across the fields that flow down to the green lane below, pointing the way home with the last of the light.

2nd February

Beneath a puddle-strewn, potholed track that bisects an arable field, a milky sun rises to hit the distant waters of the gravel pits and a song begins to drift above the familiar sounds of winter. It is muted for a time, blending into the background noise until I'm shaken into a sudden realisation of the identity of the bird, and it takes on a prominence that drowns out all competing calls.

A black pinprick set against drifting cloud is singing for all it is worth, its pitch fading in and out as it hovers high above the stubble, belting out an unbroken stream of complex melody. After months of silence, the skylarks are singing again, heralds of warmth and colour and light even as a winter chill whips my face. A few more dots come into focus, male birds hanging and calling for as long as they are able. They drop 'silver chains of sound', as George Meredith so beautifully put it in his poem *The*

Lark Ascending, the birds attempting to impress grounded females, who will pick their partners based on how long they can sustain their serenade before parachuting back down to earth.

It is thought that Ralph Vaughan Williams gained inspiration from Meredith's work. His composition of the same title, featuring a fluid, soaring violin solo, has become so familiar that, almost inevitably, it has come to be dismissed by some music critics as populist, too simple, too parochial. Perhaps I am easily pleased, but repetition has not diminished my appreciation of his exquisite score, which to my ears perfectly encapsulates the lark and all that it symbolises, reviving dormant memories of springs past, shaping notes that rise to lift the soul.

9th February

A bitter easterly wind has brought with it a dusting of snow. Although it has largely melted away by the time I manage to escape my screen for a lunchtime walk, some remains, sprinkling the corners of fields, rounding the furrows of old meadows. The cold wind plumps up robins and effortlessly slices through my winter layers. In the far distance a synchronised band of lapwing drifts over grazing greylag geese. The lapwings wheel about, their distinctive flight exaggerated by broad, paddle-shaped wings as befits a bird with a Latin name that roughly translates as 'willowing fan'. My nose feels like it matches the tight buds of lime trees, their rosy-red colour perched on the tips of dark twigs and branches.

Although the temperature is far from springlike, the balance between darkness and light feels as though it is very gradually inching towards parity, and there are signs in the village of plants beginning to awaken from dormancy, growth triggered not by warmth but by a lengthening day. Neat rosettes of shepherd's purse mix with groundsel, speedwells and poppies rising from buried seed exposed by the plough last autumn. Tiny tongue-shaped whitlowgrass leaves and spidery pearlworts have claimed bare soils, filled in gaps between pavement slabs, taken over mossy edges whilst above them the broad shiny leaves of red valerian have sprouted from greyed rootstocks firmly wedged into the gaps of stone walls.

The feathery plumes of cow parsley give structure and vibrancy to paths and verges still dominated by the brown leaves of autumn past, revving up for a dominant display in the months to follow and sharing space with the hooded tips of bluebell leaves that have cut up through the soil to form neat green clumps. Goosegrass is making its move for the light, entwined with the bleached mass of last year's growth still draped over bare hedges. The fat arrow-shaped leaves of lords-and-ladies are unfurling through apple-green carpets of moss, emerging at the bases of hedgerows and the shaded edges of trackways, as are glossy dock leaves and the first bent columns of dog's mercury, straightening towards the light in ultra-slow motion. Snowdrops in scattered green and white clusters mingle with golden winter aconite flowers balanced on pale-green ruffs. These latter two species were no doubt discarded by a gardener long ago, once unwanted but now liberated and thriving, to many a sign of the spring to come.

A far less obvious indication, but well worth searching out, are the female flowers of hazel, a collection of curled, brilliant blood-red sticky ribbons no more than a millimetre or two long, each resembling a miniature sea anemone erupting from the tip of a dull-green bud. Accompanying them and adorning the hazel's bare twigs are male catkins with yellow anthers peeking out between the parting scales, their pollen soon to be released on the wind and captured by the female's tentacles.

15th February

Cutting the corner of a pasture that traces a winding tributary flowing into the wide river beyond, a sinuous trail of flattened grass, appearing darker than the surrounding sward, betrays the regular route of an animal that leads a covert life. A loose gathering of thin black turds lies just off the path, close to the riverbank. I am not in the habit of smelling every defecation I happen across but, in this case, make an exception. It is, as I had hoped, faintly sweet-smelling but with distinctly fishy undertones. Close by, a congealed dark splodge rests on the green grass, packed full of regurgitated fish scales. There is little doubt that otters patrol this area.

The route appears to be well used and, for much of its length, spraints are deposited in varying states of decay, some now dry and grey. I follow in the otters' footsteps to a lazy willow trunk that rests along the riverbank for a couple of metres before rearing up at a right angle to peer over the water. At some point in the past the tree has lost its canopy to the wind, but like all willows it harbours Medusa-like powers and has sprouted multiple thin stems to activate the process of renewal.

The trail leads to a wide opening between the trunk and the earth, with shallow mounds of soil piled up on the grass nearby. It is not possible to see how much room has been excavated under the tree but this seems to me a perfectly respectable holt, perhaps used in drier times when there is a reduced risk of flooding. It is just possible that this is a 'couch', a safe place where an otter rests during the day, although these are almost always above ground and characterised by areas of flattened grass in much the same manner as the 'form' of a hare. As it happens, this stretch of river is used by a local angling club and I always make a point of asking if the fishing is good, and what they have caught, so I know that the otter's diet could consist of chubb, barbel, roach, dace, gudgeon, bream, roach, carp and pike. With a trout fishery and gravel pits also upstream, this location is prime otter real estate.

There are, I reckon, three main ways of going about trying to see an otter:

1. Get lucky with a completely unexpected sighting. I have twice seen an otter in twenty years of walking this area.

2. Stake out a likely spot at either dusk or just before dawn, ideally when it isn't raining, or very cold, and hope that one might appear in this small window of opportunity before darkness settles in, or the commuters start their engines.

3. Politely ask a near-neighbour who you know has a wildlife camera to set it up where there are fresh signs of otter activity and view the subsequent footage in the comfort of your living room with a nice cup of tea.

The third option is clearly not the same as seeing one 'live', but at the very least the camera footage will give clues about what time of day (or more likely night) they are most active. And it really is bitterly cold outside.

17th February

Movement breaks the beam at 6:04pm as an unnervingly large rat scuttles across a willow trunk. Eyes glowing white in infrared light, it pauses for a bit too long, staring straight into the lens, giving off faintly menacing vibes. I have been sent highlights of the camera footage and I'm hoping that this is warming me up for slightly more spectacular sightings. A stocky badger wanders past at 6:42pm and pauses to scratch at the ground. The monochrome images emphasise two perfect black stripes that run from the sides of its white snout, skimming shining eyes before broadening towards the ears and the back of the head. It's a handsome chap. Then at 7:21pm, for a few seconds, the sleek form of an otter wanders across my screen, moving towards the river, hugging the same ground where I was standing only a day before. It is wonderful to see the living form, rather than simply a trail of discarded smelly clues. The otter seems to be in rude health, to the extent that it might even be a pregnant female, although that is probably just wishful thinking.

At 2:27am, a second otter sighting. It is hard to tell if this is the same one as before, but it does look a bit slimmer in comparison. The otter scrambles over the willow trunk, heading directly towards the camera, pauses very briefly a metre of so away, then departs stage left in the direction of the pasture. The final burst of film is timed at 2:56am. Out of a static scene the otter suddenly appears from directly below the camera, face filling the screen and glowing in sepia night vision, its nose pressed against the lens, long whiskers twitching white against a black background. The camera picks up a burst of sound, somewhere between a snort and a sniff as the otter investigates the alien object. If the otter had been this close to my face I'd have been in real trouble. As it moves back towards the willow the whole body is visible for a moment, enough time to admire a lithe, streamlined build, thick wet coat and long muscular tail, before the otter is lost to the river, an apex predator on the hunt, oblivious to its new-found fame.

22nd February

A light frost has coated grassland bordering the brook, save for a soggy green ellipse that gives away the upwelling of a small spring leaking out of the earth and trickling down to a fenceline, and the river beyond. A group of fieldfares, together with a few redwings and a lone lapwing, are probing the softened soil. The thrushes hop a short distance away in a fairly nonchalant fashion as I plod past, whilst the lapwing rises a few metres into the air, circling above the springline, emitting its strange song that to my ears sounds like a malfunctioning theremin. Hearing it for the first time, you'd never guess it was produced by a bird.

A lapwing up close is a wonderful sight, especially when the sunlight strikes its plumage, and I pause to admire an iridescent green and purple sheen, the splendid wispy crest that sits on the back of its head like a jaunty haute couture hat, black paddle-shaped wing tips and a snow-white neck collar. The sight reminds me of my first attempts to photograph these birds at the edge of a lochan, stalking them through a low cover of springy bog myrtle, trying my best to blend into the background whilst a sweet resinous fragrance was released from leaves trodden underfoot.

27th February

The early morning landscape is, like me, a bit blurry-eyed, cloud and mist combining to keep the middle distance out of focus. Fields, reedbeds, trees and fencelines are reduced to smudged shapes and block design. A hidden song thrush sings out brief loops of its impressive repertoire, clear flautist notes drifting up to meet the silhouettes of a skein of honking greylag geese set against a blank canvas, the troop infiltrated by a comically small mallard nestled into their V-shape formation, flapping its wings in double-time. Profiles of tufted ducks, gadwall, teal and wigeon glide on the still surface of the gravel pits, whistling waters blending with a chalky sky.

By mid afternoon, definition has been restored and cold easterly winds have changed to pleasing south-westerlies. Mud again replaces frozen soils, gloves and woolly hat remaining buried in my jacket pocket. Two kites glide above and past a row of alders lining the river's edge. The birds are clasping thin branches in their talons, heading for giant sequoias to begin the process of patching up last year's nest. It is a striking example of the influence of humans on the local landscape; the tree a native to coastal regions of California and Oregon, saplings shipped and planted here in the mid 19th century by Victorian enthusiasts, and the bird extinct by the time the trees were fresh in the soil now returned, the two species combining to create a novel 21st-century scene which is in parts both natural and man-made.

On my way home I spot the dog sniffing something up ahead in the corner of an arable field that is usually too wet in the spring and early summer for a crop to flourish, the ground sown instead with grasses and herbs that produce copious quantities of seed for birds to feast on in the barren months. He doesn't come to me when I call – not an unusual state of affairs, but there is something suspicious about his behaviour – so I walk up to see what has caught his attention. A sparrowhawk lies motionless, leathered yellow talons curled in, barred belly showing, its feathers damp and dirty. Chocolate-brown wings that once struck fear into songbirds are now stiff and still. There are no obvious signs of how the bird came to rest here, although it no longer has its head, so it is unlikely to stage a comeback. If I had seen a pigeon in this state, suspicion would fall on a peregrine. Perhaps it simply expired due to old age, or hunger. Maybe the head is considered a delicacy in vulpine circles.

As I casually ponder the inevitability of death, the dog, free from the burden of existential angst, rolls on the dead bird. He seems to enjoy rolling on dead things, the worst by far being an incident while on holiday in Northumberland when we found him rubbing against the decomposing body of a grey seal washed up on the shoreline within sight of Lindisfarne Castle. The drive home to our rented cottage was not a pleasant one. I quickly pull him back from the hawk, a robin sings out a wonderfully upbeat melody from a nearby hedge, and the dog moves on to the entrance of a large rabbit burrow and the promise of fresh, juicy pellets.

1st March

A blackbird acts as a very effective if slightly unwelcome alarm call in the half-light, belting out its dual-purpose song, calling for a mate whilst protecting its territory. It is the first day of meteorological spring and although the sights, sounds and scents of two seasons have begun to overlap, chilly north-easterlies are back, temporarily blowing away the recent promise of prolonged warmth.

Chattering flocks of fieldfares remain, reluctant to leave their wintering grounds. Queen bumblebees have begun to emerge, searching out early sources of nectar to refuel after months of solitary hibernation. Along paths and field edges, clumps of shining celandines mix with patches of fresh buttercups sitting under budding blackthorn. Slender green shoots of reed and sedge have appeared through brown decomposing debris. Trilling long-tailed tits weave through the hedges, picking and feeding as they go. Wigeon, goldeneye and teal that have grazed the wet grasslands since late autumn will soon be off to their northern breeding grounds.

But it is the sound drifting up from the water meadows that stops me in my tracks. The haunting call of a curlew, returned much earlier than in years past, permeates the cold wind, loosening winter's grip. Twirling, burbling notes reach a crescendo that reverberates over the river and fields, rising above all other sounds. Its song speaks of persistence, of ancient landscapes. It fills me with joy, with pride, with hope.

4th March

Hibernating memories of springs past are gradually awakened. Over the past few days, I have seen my first pipistrelle bat of the year appear out of a steel-blue evening light, patrolling the garden fenceline and passing just a metre or two in front of me and my 6pm beer. The first tiny insect has flown into my eye, an event that long ago became part of my 'almost spring' signage. Tiny white flowers of whitlowgrass are again flecking wall tops and the edges of pavements. Sweet violets lend their colour and subtle scent to verges and back lanes. The first impatient hawthorn and elder leaves have unfurled, whilst butter-yellow brimstone butterflies flutter in air heavy with the smell of freshly mown grass.

Such seasonal firsts are usually triggered by temperature or light, or both, and whilst the former may fluctuate considerably from year to year, with a global thermostat increasingly regulated by us, the latter is constant, ruled by the tilting of the Earth's axis. Not even late-lying snow or bitter winds can turn the tide of steadily lighter mornings, lengthening evenings and a sun that hangs higher in the sky. In fact, the number of hours of daylight speeds up at this time of year, peaking during the spring equinox before slowing down around the solstices, forming on paper a pleasing S-shaped curve. Not only does increased day length make us more alert, it is to some as effective in treating seasonal depression as prescription drugs. As much as I relish the 'firsts' of the season, it is the changing light that lifts me out of winter.

In a sheltered spot the warming sun catches my face and tilts back my head, compelling me to stand motionless, eyes closed and arms outstretched to bask like a lemur.

10th March

Not all birds sing sweet melodies to attract a mate. Both male and female great spotted woodpeckers use an iron-like beak to advertise their location and availability, rapping on dead wood high up in the canopy. Their staccato drumming resonates across open fields as I make my way down to the water meadows. My heart sinks as I spot a scuffed brown linear strip about 10m long and 3m wide standing out amidst the neatly cropped grassland. Clods of turf have been torn up, turned over and cast either side of the broken ridge. Nearby, I find numerous small, scuffed-up rounded pits a few centimetres deep, seemingly formed by burrowing noses searching out food beneath the surface. These are known as 'snuffle holes' and, together with the state of the ridge, suggest that badgers have been busy here.

But in fact, a closer examination at this scene of destruction, and of the manner in which the turf has been torn, reveals that the badger has been set up as a fall guy by gangs of rooks and crows. The corvids are, rather incredibly, able to detect hidden food by listening out for the faint sound of beetle larvae feeding and burrowing underground. The birds then use their powerful pickaxe beaks to rip away the grass, exposing soil that harbours juicy delicacies such as the plump grubs of the cockchafer beetle, which develop underground for four or five years before emerging as adults. Also known as maybugs, for a few weeks in late spring and early summer these deeply impressively insects take to the air, outer casings opening like a 1980's DeLorean to expose a blur of wings that often propel its bumbling bulk unnervingly close to your head. Although the innocent name of the cockchafer roughly translates as 'big beetle' in Old English, I always delight in the sniggers that greet its name by the uninitiated.

The small patch of grassland will recover. It takes more than a few crows to displace deep-rooted perennials, and who knows, seeds of a few species that were waiting for the opportunity to spring from the seed bank may also fill the gaps, given time.

Further downstream, mature alders are shaking off their winter torpor. Hundreds of thousands of compact catkins are beginning to unlock and expand, a gradual articulation revealing minute flowers and a mass of pollen between purple scales that slowly transforms canopies from mauve to shades of ochre and chartreuse. When fully open, the male catkins are three times the length of their winter form. I study the detail of a flower, the pollen held on anthers painting my fingertips yellow. Tapping catkins dangling from branches within reach produces fine yellow clouds that hang and drift around my head. The female catkins sit above the males and are much smaller, only a centimetre or two long. In time they will transform into the small, round, blackened cones that still cling onto branches after last year's pollination event. Most females will flower in a few weeks' time and are best appreciated magnified by a hand lens, revealing translucent burgundy-red stigmas snaking out from behind rough, dark-brown scales. Alder is the dominant tree growing by this section of riverbank, its roots able to tolerate prolonged periods in waterlogged soils. It stands to reason that Venice is largely built upon foundations constructed from this water-resistant timber.

As I stroll on, my peripheral vision catches a bird flying over the field. Its size and flight at first remind me of the woodpecker I heard drumming earlier, wings held tight to its body between beats so that its flight trajectory has a dipping, bouncing rhythm. It lands a short distance away, perched in an upright posture high above in a sunlit alder canopy. I have my binoculars with me and after a few minutes of searching, make out a pale face with a dark brown streak behind the eye. Changing position to get a better view of the whole bird, there is an obvious and profuse spotting[26] on its large cream breast. It has a small, very neat head and beak, a slightly pot-bellied body, a long straight tail and a brown back that, with the sun behind it, appears almost slate-grey. The bird preens for a while, then stretches its neck to reach for something, perhaps an insect hidden within a catkin. The penny finally drops. It is a mistle thrush, our largest songbird but one I rarely see. It starts to sing, its beak when viewed in my binoculars opening a fraction before the sound reaches my ears. Its song is a beautiful, lilting melody with a rather melancholic tone, which I later read is due to its preference for singing in a minor key. The mistle thrush has many different names in folklore, perhaps the most well-known being 'stormcock', as not even the dirtiest wet and windy weather stops it from

---

[26] When seen clearly, these spots appear as downward pointing arrows

performing. Amongst the many alternative nicknames for the mistle thrush, my favourite is 'Big Mary', although I have no idea of the origin. Sometimes a name just sticks.

14th March

The transformation of our village arteries is underway. Dark green, purple-edged elder leaves mix with the fresh apple-green of hawthorn, filling out winter gaps. Whilst ash and oak continue to wait patiently, neighbouring wych elms are in bloom. They display a mass of wine-red flowers, like miniature pom-poms, sitting on thin twigs set off at right angles from the main branches. I reach up to bend a branch down to eye-level and get a closer look at the collection of protruding dark-purple anthers, soon to split open to release their pollen and, with luck, meet with a nearby receptive female stigma. The continuing disastrous effects of Dutch elm disease means that some trees stand out from the crowd. Deprived of water and nutrients and so of bark, buds and flowers, their branches have become brittle, cloaked in golden and mint-green lichens, their bare skeletons fixed and weathered.

An impressively large flock of fieldfares passes above arable fields as I make my way down to the gravel pits. They are leaving their wintering grounds en masse to the songs of skylarks and the terrestrial accompaniment of robins, the latter's melody changed from the melancholic tune of months past to something much louder and more cheerful as the males begin to advertise their credentials to potential mates. As I reach the wooden bridge that spans the brook marking the boundary to the reserve, a large group of small dark shapes coast into the willows and alders that line the waterside, flitting from one tree to the next. They are a gregarious, noisy lot, emitting an idiosyncratic electronic zapping call which my phone app tells me belongs to the redpoll, a lovely bird with a distinctive red crown and a washed-out pink chest. I eventually manage to get close enough with my binoculars to match the image I'm seeing in front of me with the one displayed on my small flat screen. I was quite a late adopter of this type of technology, fearing its constant distraction, but it has become a valuable if not always infallible assistant.

Crossing over the bridge and heading west, long-tailed tits weave through hedgerows, picking and feeding as they go. The scattered plantings of cherry plum along the brookside are in leaf and flower, long hair-like anthers shooting out from a centre surrounded by six white petals, and behind them delicate green oval sepals bending back towards the branch. The white blossoms attract bands of honeybees, flies and queen bumblebees, the latter's bulk bending thin twigs as they land to feed. The blossoms of cherry plum are frequently mistaken for blackthorn, which is our dominant hedgerow shrub, but the latter tends to come into flower a good two or three weeks later. The differences between these two close relatives are subtle but clear when the shape of the sepals, the size of the petals and the length of the flower stalk are closely examined, but no matter what the identification, the mass of white plumes held on dark stems offers a welcome sight.

Further along the path I bump into a birdwatcher carrying a large, expensive-looking telescope who asks in a friendly manner if I've seen 'the glossy ibis', her glinting eyes giving away the enthusiasm of one who is in search of a rarity. The bird has been here for weeks, apparently. I am not exactly sure what it looks like – a negative image of a little egret, I think. I have to disappoint her, and although I have no real intention of actively seeking it out, a bit of the thrill of the chase is transferred to me by some kind of twitcher osmosis. I am advised to look for a group of people staring into the distance, rather than trying to spot the bird myself. Somewhere out there, the ibis is wandering around, oblivious to the excitement it has generated.

Many different willow species line the brook but all are still in bud save for one, the goat willow.[27] This is a common species of damp areas, separating itself from the pack at this time of the year by revealing soft catkins bursting out from behind olive-green scales. Caught in the sunlight, the young catkins have a captivating silver-white sheen, which, when I manipulate one between my fingers, changes colour from green to grey then back to shining silver. Their look and feel triggers memories of a friend at primary school showing a group of us a 'lucky' rabbit foot that he carried around for a while in his pocket. His tall tales of how he came by the foot amazed and repulsed us in equal measure, although I suspected at the time that his story involving snares and bowie knives was probably not entirely true, especially as the base of the astonishingly soft and tactile appendage was encircled with an ornate silver collar.

Turning for home, on a whim I step inside one of the bird hides, close to where I was told about the ibis. The indoor space is empty. I open the wooden shutters, sit

[27] Also known as 'sallow'

down on narrow slats, raise my binoculars, look in the general direction of a group of geese near to the edge of the water and immediately spot a polished black bird with a long, curved bill. It is feeding by the edge of a shallow ditch that runs to the flooded pit, poking the soft earth for tasty morsels, sharing ground with a great white egret and a few boisterous gulls. As the ibis turns to catch the sunlight, its coat transforms from a shining black to iridescent purples and greens. It really is very beautiful. I admire it for a few minutes before something unseen disturbs the gulls, the ibis gives a quick flap of its wings, I see the glossy plumage one last time, black and purple and green and russet brown all flashing on and off, before it dips down into the belly of the ditch, out of sight. I am certain that if I had travelled here to purposefully track it down, I would have failed. Emerging from the hide I greet only the second person I have seen today. He is wearing binoculars and carrying a large, expensive-looking telescope. I let him know about the ibis in as nonchalant a way as I can muster and he thanks me profusely. I was probably beaming from ear to ear.

18th March

Near to where a tarmac road stops and the green lane starts off towards the woodland, a pasture is alive with the high-pitched bleating of lambs, just a couple of weeks old and freshly turned out. The much deeper, authoritative call of their mothers keeps most of the lambs close, although some young renegades use their new-found freedom to push the boundaries, hanging out at the base of an old oak, one of them climbing onto a ledge jutting out from its thick knotted base, king of the castle. In amongst this pastoral scene, jackdaws searching for nesting material strut around the field, picking up beaks-full of fleece discarded on the grass by ewes scratching away their winter coat. At the far end of the field, I watch as a few lambs burst from a standing start into a sprint, flushing out starlings feeding in the long grass. Gangly legs skip and kick, occasionally propelling the lambs into a vertical take-off, as if they have stepped on a live electric wire, springing snow-white bodies into the crisp morning air. Maybe their actions are purely instinctive, a way of testing limitations, but it is hard not to think that what they are feeling now is something approaching pure joy.

As the dog and I splash past dunnocks calling from within the blackthorn hedges lining both sides of the lane, sections of which have white flower buds almost ready to erupt, a male yellowhammer finds the highest vantage point, tilts back his head and repeats a refrain over fields of cabbage-green winter oilseed rape stretching into the distance. Yellowhammers are striking birds, with russet-brown plumage flowing into a canary-yellow head and belly. Viewed up close, a few dashes of brown can be seen amid the yellow, adding vibrancy through contrast. The timbre and rhythm of their song is often interpreted as the mnemonic 'a-little-bit-of-bread-and-no-cheeeese', which actually fits quite nicely, though any memorable phrase to accompany the rapid string of five to eight notes, ending with a single drawn-out tone, will do, as long as it sticks. In some areas where reason was in short supply, some misguided folk once believed that the song matched the rather sinister phrase 'may-the-devil-take-yooou', apparently under the misapprehension that the yellowhammer was partial to drinking the devil's blood and retaining a drop on its tongue as proof of this heinous act (the fact that there is no red spot on the tongue didn't seem to matter). A more harmless animal it is hard to imagine, but mud sticks and the yellowhammer was persecuted due to this nonsensical association.

The yellowhammer actually has another call up its sleeve (wing?), occasionally emitting a sharp and vaguely electronic 'dzip' sound. It is possible that they use this alternative, much less flamboyant call to avoid being detected by predators when out in open countryside, while still subtly advertising their territory, letting their bright colouration do most of the work. Or it might be purely an alarm call. Nobody seems to know. The reason for its unusual name, however, requires less detective work. It is a bunting, and the Anglo-Saxon word for bunting is 'ammer'. Although like most birds, the yellowhammer has a variety of colloquial names, perhaps the most elegant being the 'writing lark' in reference to the fine inky lines and scribbles that adorn the smooth surface of its eggs. We might view such miraculously complex patterns as aesthetically beautiful, but they serve a very real purpose for the bird. Not only does the 'writing' act as a kind of camouflage, but the yellowhammer has the ability to discriminate between its own signature and that of the handwriting of a master forger, the cuckoo.

21st March

My phone celebrates the spring equinox by sending me a link so that I can reminisce about what happened on this day, thirteen years ago. In the photos there is deep snow outside the house and my daughters are being pulled around on sledges. Today a ground frost has taken me slightly by surprise, but a white-out seems unlikely this morning as the wintry veneer rapidly retreats from a warming sun that has passed the celestial equator.

In the pasture that abuts our garden, a common grass-like plant that hides in plain sight for much of the year has cast off its anonymity. Held above narrow leaves and thin flower-stalks lined with straggly white hairs sit mops of lemon-yellow anthers surrounded by a star-shaped cluster of shiny, pointed, dark-brown nutlets. This diminutive plant protrudes just a few centimetres above the turf but in such numbers that once noticed they are present wherever I step. Field woodrush, also known as Good Friday grass, is a welcome sight, a faithful indicator marking not just the start of spring but the resurrection of grasslands that will soon be flushed with new colour and life.

By early afternoon the temperature has hit the mid-teens. I walk up to the brow of the hill where arable meets woodland. To my left the land rolls down to an extensive thicket of goat willow. Hundreds of catkins adorn each tree, and collectively the canopies are lit up by countless millions of beads of golden pollen, a feast for freshly emerging insects in the days and weeks to follow.

I am welcomed into the wood by the sweet scent of spring, by brimstone and small tortoiseshell butterflies and the familiar call of a raven high up in the pines. As I stroll leisurely along a wide sunny ride, evenly spaced conifers to one side and leggy hazel coppice on the other, a rustling sound draws my gaze down to the south-facing edge of the path and I catch the briefest sight of two silvery-grey tails slithering into the undergrowth. After a winter spent hibernating, slow worms have resurfaced. Their common name is rather misleading, as they are actually not a worm, or even a snake, but rather a lizard that has lost its legs. They are not particularly slow either. The ones that I disturb flee from their suntrap at a fair pace, but if you do happen across one and see it before it sees you, look at the eyes, and more specifically notice its eyelids, a feature that is absent from snakes.

After a time, my first chiffchaff of the year comes into view, freshly arrived from the Mediterranean basin where it has spent the autumn and winter months. As the bird flits between branches edging a scalloped glade, I am close enough, with binoculars in hand, to see a pale streak above its eye as it sings out its eponymous two-note, see-saw call. It is a song that will be ever present in the landscape for months to come, replacing the recently departed 'chack-chack' of the fieldfare.

The chiffchaffs sing. A brimstone butterfly drifts over flowering blackthorn. As I pause to take in these welcome sights and sounds, bathing in a wide warming beam, a brilliant flash of colour rushes past, three magnificent male bullfinches illuminated by the sun, their shining black heads and brilliant coral-pink breasts popping against a background of neutral browns and greys.

This unexpected sight elevates what is fast turning into a memorable day. It is little wonder that bullfinches were so coveted by 19th century collectors, a prized captive bird whose beautiful plumage and call could be admired at leisure by the 'owners'. As misguided as this practice was, there were worse things that could happen to a bullfinch, especially if it was unlucky enough to be caught eating the flower buds of pears, plums or apples by the owner of an orchard. The collection and possession of wild birds such as finches has been outlawed for over 40 years, though protection is a relative term for the bullfinch, as it is, rather incredibly, still possible to apply for a licence to shoot them if they are perceived to be causing damage to a fruit crop.

A brim-full pond sits a few hundred metres up ahead, the same pond where I heard the cuckoo's first call last year. For a second spring running I conduct a fruitless search for frogspawn. Scuffed-up banks imprinted with deer tracks suggest it has been a popular watering hole in recent weeks. I wait for a while in anticipation of the cuckoo, but know deep down that I'm too early. The absence of frogspawn may be linked with the predatory great crested newts living in the muddy depths, who will soon begin wrapping their eggs in the leaves of aquatic vegetation. I consider returning in a few weeks to search other ponds deeper within the wood, just in case there are any toads in the vicinity, as, like the adults their offspring have a poisonous gland behind the eye and so, in theory, fare better than frog tadpoles in a world of predators. Still, there is no sense of disappointment. There must be ample habitat around where frogs stand a chance of success, and the walk was more than worth it for the brief, unexpected glimpse of slow worms, the stunning bullfinches, the welcome return of chiffchaffs and the simple pleasures of walking in a wood bursting into spring.

27th March

Sitting on a comfy sofa with my first cup of coffee in hand, I watch a pair of resident dunnocks busy in the back garden cleaning up the flower beds, hopping and pecking around clumps of camassias, alliums and bluebells. The birds split up to explore mossy gaps between paving stones and nearby plant pots. One of them seems overly disconcerted by its reflection in the shiny surface of a pot, possibly believing the mirror image to be a rival. It dances around the glaze, wings whirring, beak poised, ready for combat with this bold upstart. It eventually gives up, either exhausted by the stamina of its nemesis, or happy that it has done its best to secure territory. The birds soon move on to a wilder border that hangs on to last year's dead flower stems, searching out insects, small spiders and the odd worm or two. It is possible that they are the same birds that appear to be constructing a nest in the privet hedge that wraps around our front garden, which is a good reminder to leave any trimming until the end of July at the earliest. It is a task I can happily delay.

Also known as the hedge sparrow (although technically, it is not a sparrow at all, but an accentor), the dunnock has a smoky blue-grey face, breast and underwings and, much like the house sparrow, a mixture of pale buff and darker brown streaks covering the rest of its body. It is often dismissed as a dull bird, but whilst the dunnock does admittedly have a rather understated beauty, its love life is not nearly as restrained. Once regarded by Victorians as an exemplar of fidelity, recent research involving genetic fingerprinting and paternity analysis has shown that things are not quite as conventional as they once appeared. Although some pairs do live a monogamous life if there is no competition for territory, their usual behaviour is far more complex, involving either polyandry, meaning that a female will attempt to mate with at least two males, or polygamy, with a male sharing several females. At the height of courtship, dunnocks may mate with each other up to fifty times a day, enough to make the most liberal of Victorians blush. A male will attempt to ensure that he, rather than his rivals, successfully passes on his genes via the extraordinary practice of pecking the female's cloaca. This causes her to eject the sperm of the previous partner, although paternity issues are usually left unsettled and so the male birds share feeding duties, not knowing if the chicks are theirs or not but erring on the side of caution. This in turn significantly increases the chances of the brood being raised successfully.

Such complex behaviour has at its heart the notion of a female taking control of her sex life to ensure the quality and diversity of her progeny. Although Darwin recognised the importance of female choice as a driving force in sexual selection, its influence on evolution was neglected (or actively resisted) until very recently, in large part due to the significant imbalance in the gender of the scientists researching the subject (i.e., they were mostly male) and the subsequent choice of study and interpretation of findings. It is no coincidence that as the gender balance in science has shifted, different questions have been asked, resulting in an evidence-base that has become more pluralistic and which has, rather predictably, substantively advanced our understanding of evolutionary biology and behaviour. It is possibly stretching it a bit to say that our contemporary understanding of the dunnock encapsulates the progression of societal norms, but I think it is fair to say that the dunnock is far from dull.

1st April

Just past midday I escape the desk to stretch my legs and stroll down to the brook to check for frog- or toadspawn, having had no luck in the woodland pond a couple of weeks ago. On the way I bump into a friend, who tells me that only yesterday she saw a big fat toad in the very field I'm heading towards. Perhaps I share some kind of affinity with toads, that we are both drawn to the same area at the same time. Some cultures believe in a 'spirit animal', although I must say I had hoped for a slightly more glamorous-looking associate.

Stone walls that act as boundary markers for gardens, the school playground and open fields are now softened with an abundance of flowering life. Henbit and red deadnettles, field and ivy-leaved speedwells, ivy-leaved toadflax, biting stonecrop, flattened meadow-grass, grape hyacinth, groundsel, trailing lobelia, wavy bittercress, shining cranesbill and the pea-green seed pods of whitlowgrass have all found their own niche within the complex jigsaw that forms the vertical faces or the upturned 'cock and hen' slabs that crown the tops. Their roots do no harm to the integrity of the wall and their flowers weave colour and interest, as well as providing food and shelter for a wide variety of freshly emerged insects; even so, a few homeowners still habitually cleanse sections with a liberal application of herbicide. Tidiness is no friend to wildlife.

Just now, the star of the stonework is the delicate rue-leaved saxifrage, its flowers beginning to open, tiny white petals held above trident-shaped leaves, the whole plant no more than a couple of centimetres across and covered in fine, sticky, glandular hairs. In our area it is a specialist of walls held together with a lime-based mortar, but in its more 'natural' habitats it is a plant of wild dune grassland, limestone pavement and rock ledges. By building the walls, we have inadvertently created a perfect environment for the plant, and it has taken full advantage of our generosity.

The songs of sparrows, yellowhammers and the now ubiquitous chiffchaffs follow me out of the village, down to verges flushed golden yellow with the glossy eight-petalled flowers of lesser celandine, growing with matt mauve ground ivy and deep-violet and white clumps of sweet violet. Somewhere within this fresh scene, glow-worm larvae are feeding on slugs and snails. A few sections of south-facing blackthorn hedge are in flower, but the full display is perhaps a week off, black branches adorned with countless pearl-like buds. I cross over the road, into the pasture, over a barbed fence and head down to the narrow, shaded brook, brushing through shin-high cow parsley.

The brook is in places just a trickle, running over algae- and moss-covered pebbles, many of which are scarred with the squiggled memories of caddis fly larvae. Fool's watercress, water mint and brooklime grow in shallow sections but there is no sign of the long, beaded strings of toadspawn anchored to rooted stems. I continue upstream and disturb something that darts beneath the surface, perhaps a stickleback. The movement draws my eye away from the spot I was scanning, and towards two large clumps of frogspawn in one of the deeper sections of the brook I had just walked past. Sometimes you can't see for looking. Each clump has hundreds of milky globes, one jellied egg linked to the next, the whole mass attached to pebbles half hidden in the depths. The spawn has clearly been here for a while, for the opaque eggs are covered with a fine dusting of silt. Some still have tiny formative black dots cocooned within, a closer inspection revealing motionless black heads and tails, but the majority of tadpoles have hatched and lie against their punctured casings, feeding on the remains of the jelly and building up reserves of energy for the final great escape.

As my feet become cold, I realise that water is overtopping my boots. I move a few paces backwards to a raised area and see two more clumps of frogspawn, almost precisely where I started my search, and then a toad, perfectly still next to the spawn. It is very definitely a toad, well-camouflaged brown-olive colours matching almost exactly the colour of the sediment that dominates the surface of the brook. It takes a few seconds before I remember my binoculars are hanging around my neck. I focus in and see clearly its wrinkled, warty back, slightly pale snout and bright golden eyes, the colour of a rising sun, looking sideways in my direction. It is sitting with front limbs outstretched in a rather formidable pose. The combination of clumps of spawn with a toad nearby temporarily confuses me, but it is simply coincidence rather than an elaborate, toad-based April Fool. After all, why shouldn't a fellow amphibian share the same waters?

The half-submerged lonesome toad, probably sensing danger, kicks his long back legs and swims over to the nearest cluster of frogspawn. It stretches out its front limbs around the mass of eggs in what could be interpreted as a protective gesture, or even a hug. But it is neither. The toad is simply trying to hide. I decide to leave it in peace and make a mental note to come back periodically to check on the tadpoles' progress. Sitting on the bankside, I remove my wellies and wring out sodden socks. I'm delighted to have found frogspawn, slightly frustrated that I didn't discover evidence of toads breeding, but hopeful that somewhere nearby, perhaps in a garden pond, they have been successful in passing on their genes to the next generation.

6th April

Standing at the river's edge, scanning the expanse of water meadow beyond, in my binoculars I see a hare move amongst dark, geese-grazed patches of jointed rush. I follow its lolloping motion out of the rushes and into a lighter green where jackdaws are feeding, the white of its tail flashing against russet fur. Nearby a second hare lies still, its marbled form hunkered down, black-tipped ears pinned flat against its back. Standing water marking out a shallow depression a few hundred metres from the river bank is speckled white with the bodies of black-headed gulls. In the foreground, so close that I can rest my binoculars and still see them clearly, two curlews balance on pencil-thin legs, their bodies charcoal-grey in this light, necks and dark downward-curved bills rather awkwardly twisted to undertake essential preening. Then suddenly, in one swift movement, the birds crouch low, their sizable wingspans are revealed, legs straighten and they launch into the air. The curlews arc over the meadow, landing close to where I first spotted the hare, the male calling out in a twirling, upward inflection. Settled amongst the cropped rushes their heads and bills begin to nod back and forth like pumpjacks, probing the soft earth in search of buried prey.

The margins sing out with the scratchy songs of returning blackcaps, whitethroats, sedge and reed warblers alongside the cascading notes of willow warblers, all abruptly drowned out for a few seconds by thunderous bursts from a Cetti's warbler, ever present in our parish but silent in the winter months and always hidden from view. The first waves of house martins and swallows speed overhead, shrill calls magically restored from the African plains, their epic journey impossible to comprehend. In the past, men of science would argue over whether these birds spent the autumn and winter months on the moon, or submerged in the muddy depths of riverbeds. Every so often a swallow brakes with wings outstretched, turning on a sixpence to ensnare its quarry. The wind whips up a thick band of reed that forms a taupe barrier between me and the river, rustling last year's dry stems that hold plumed heads packed with seeds retained in soft white down, a few escaping to drift on the currents they reveal.

11th April

The hedgerow elms, not long ago in flower, now hold prolific numbers of seeds. They cluster together, each one centred and gift-wrapped in a wafer-thin oval casing resembling an insect's wing. Scrambling below them, tangled swathes of bramble are dressed with fresh, glossy three-lobed leaves, providing cover for the birds that have begun to nest within its protected realm. Hawthorn and elder have formed tiny tight flower buds, easily missed amongst fresh foliage, but not for long. Elongated rose whips arch from the tops of hedges to dangle over footpaths, waiting to snag the unwary traveller's head. The broad buds of field maple are curled back like planed wood shavings, revealing smooth leaves and delicate upright flower stalks. They mingle in the hedgerow with the first neat, crinkled leaves of hazel that in the weeks to follow will grow to four times their current size. The final few gaps are being filled, but the obvious splendour in the landscape is not green but white.

Blackthorn is, by its nature, a plant of the margins. Belonging to the cherry family, it spreads horizontally by a suckering rootstock and, if left unchecked, may soon develop dense thickets. The flowers appear before the leaves and bundled together form long drifts of clean white blooms on bare black branches. They attract a few insects that I recognise and a multitude of others that I do not. Each flower is held tight to the twig, with five wafer-thin petals clasped flat around a central green ring. Rising up from this centre are numerous anthers, hair-like filaments stuck like pins in a cushion, balancing tiny blobs of lemon-yellow pollen at their tips, a few already spent and turned a light rust or brick-red colour. The flowers encircle and tightly pack the twigs in dense rings overlapping each other, and the abundance of anthers set against this white background lends a slightly hazy, out-of-focus appearance to each full branch. I count about fifty flowers on a five-centimetre section. The sizeable thicket in front of me must collectively hold millions.

Boulder clay soils overlying limestone bedrock provide the perfect growing conditions for blackthorn to flourish here, and at peak flowering time its presence is obvious far into the distance. On the horizon, dense white plumes contrast with a backdrop of evergreen conifers and a naked jumble of oak and ash, exposing the protective barrier encircling the woodland. In the middle distance, kilometres of neat chunky hedgerow flailed last autumn display a complex morse code of green where hawthorn and elder grow, and a pure white where the blackthorn blooms. Along the footpath that links our village with the next, thorn flowers tumble down into wild wet woodland.

Protected from a wind-chill sweeping the exposed fields, as the clouds part and the temperature rises, blackcap, wren, robin and chiffchaff sing out from secret places, and the blackthorn dazzles. For much of today it has been too cold to get even the faintest whiff of the flower's delicate almond scent, even when I have buried my nose deep within its blooms, but as the sun warms this sheltered spot their subtle perfume begins to infuse the air. The flowers are also said to have a slight almondy taste if eaten, although it is probably not advisable to consume them in any great quantity, given that the sweet taste of these compounds can be converted by the human body into cyanide when digested.

I have scrambled through enough woodlands to know how deeply unpleasant an experience being lost in a blackthorn thicket can be. It has fierce thorns that, if they puncture the skin, are not only painful but can result in a severe reaction. Indeed, the 'crown of thorns' so cruelly used for the crucifixion is said by some to have been constructed from blackthorn, epitomising the dark undertones that have been associated with this species for millennia. We tend to demonise the things that we perceive as being harmful, but blackthorn's fearsome reputation to us is one of the principal reasons for it being such a beneficial plant for so much wildlife, its dense growth habitat, impenetrable armour and abundant nectar providing shelter, nourishment and protection.

Whilst blackthorn in April can't quite match the magnificent spectacle of the 'sakura' cherry blossom adorning its larger-flowered, more glamorous (and much less hazardous) cousins over in Japan, such a wonderful mass-flowering event so close to home might provide us with similar moments of reflection on the transitory existence of all life, and a greater appreciation of the natural world that we live within and depend upon.

16th April

There is a plant that should be in full bloom now, an ancient tree in the same family as the blackthorn. It requires a trip to the edge of the woodland, to the north-eastern edge of the village boundary, and I set off almost as soon as I arrive home from an early morning dog walk, brushing past holly blue butterflies investigating the hedge outside our front door. I cycle with chiffchaffs, yellowhammers and skylarks, past a farmer with plough at the ready, pedalling slowly but steadily up to the woodland edge where I look down over the expanse of sallow, its canopy now a fresh sage green. A buzzard nearby heaves itself off the ground and into flight, the effort expended showing it to be a sturdier, more powerful bird than the relatively lightweight red kite. Watching it steadily quartering the skies as I catch my breath, with effortless ease it straightens to coast on a single beat of its wings as far as I could walk in an hour.

The white buds of crab apple, washed rose pink at their edges, mass at the entrance. A thick trunk coppiced in the past is rooted to an ancient woodbank, flowers open where the top of the canopy touches blue sky. A few of the apple's leaves are dusted a striking candyfloss-pink, evidence of a benign infection caused by a minuscule mite. A woodpecker drums in the distance. Just on from the apple is a sign notifying me that forestry works are taking place within the wood. The notice warns in stark cartoon-like images of an imminent danger of death, but fails to inform me where or how this might happen. Mortality noted, I push on up a steep, sun-baked ride, pause halfway to take in dawn chorus stragglers, and remember that I left my binoculars on the kitchen table.

The branches of an oak reach out to meet the centre of the ride and I am delighted to see leaves, though only just. Translucent wavy-edged shapes smaller than my thumbnail crowd the tips of branches, many still emerging from their chestnut-brown casings. The lobed margins of each leaf have a fine down of white hairs, as do the scales of the parting buds. Whilst I may not have my binoculars, I find my hand lens in a trouser pocket, far more useful in the circumstances. I hold a leaf between my thumb and forefinger, hold it up to the light, bring the leaf towards the lens and my eye. Its surface is paper thin, supported structurally by a central vein with secondary veins branching off at regular intervals, the pattern created on the leaf resembling the simplified architecture of the tree's long-familiar winter form. An intricate network of much finer veins loops and connects to create irregular polygons, plumbed in to provide nutrients, water and energy to the tree for the coming months. The transformation of this individual, from bare branches to buds and then leaves, has been played out for more than three hundred springs and might continue for another three hundred. When it was as old as I will ever live to be, its canopy was over ten metres above the spot where an acorn fell and germinated. George III was on the throne, the fields below this wood were being partitioned by Enclosure Acts and Napoleon was sweeping across much of continental Europe, about to face his literal Waterloo. Hanging around a mature oak tends to lend a degree of perspective.

The central forestry track cutting the woodland in two has recently been resurfaced with rubble and sand compacted to create a solid, slightly cambered and very smooth surface, more road now than track to ease the movement of heavy machinery that occasionally roams the area, extracting timber. The wide surface, virtually bare save for a scattering of blackthorn confetti, is in stark contrast to the colour and complexity of the edge flora and the jumble of shrubs and trees that line the way. I coast along this incongruously clean, snaking line for a while before turning off onto a narrow juddery ride towards the target for the morning, scattering basking peacock butterflies as I go. The woodland comes to an abrupt end, exposing a vast pale sky above hay meadows liberally peppered with dandelions and cowslips. One more step and I'll be outside the village boundary, but I can see the trees from here, a wall of blossom towering above a blackthorn hedge. The wild pears are at their glorious best.

While the blackthorn is a blur of fine white, the considerably larger pear flowers are arranged in relatively discrete clumps, as if dabbed onto the trees with the tip of an impressionist's brush. A buzzing sound begins to usurp birdsong as I approach the pears and stand under their wide canopies, the flowers and the spaces in between alive with the traffic of bees, beetles, wasps and flies, lots of flies, feeding and pollinating, setting in motion the creation of small green orbicular fruits that will ripen in late summer. The flowers, about three times the size of those of the blackthorn, have five white petals connected by a central star of light green sepals. A single green stigma rises from its centre and is surrounded by splendid burgundy anthers nestled within the slightly cupped bloom. Groups of about twelve flowers, all emanating from a single point and held on stout pedicels, assemble above a whorl of oval leaves sporting a down to their edges and undersides. The leaves and flowers are positioned on the tips of secondary twigs only a few centimetres long and growing at an angle of about 90 degrees from the main branch. They adorn twisting, dark-brown trunks close to two metres thick and rising 12m from the nourishing earth.

After studying the flowers for a while, I begin to notice their scent. I had forgotten how unpleasant it is, slightly fishy and a complete contrast from their bridal posy appearance, although the hundreds of pollinators flocking to the pear suggest that the tree is not at all bothered about my sense of smell. I sit a suitable distance away to eat my lunch, which is rather miraculously still untouched. A male orange tip butterfly flutters past, proclaiming spring. It lands on the white cross-shaped flowers of garlic mustard, staying just long enough for me to admire dazzling orange wingtips and mottled moss-green undersides, before it is hustled on by a slightly larger green-veined white, it too in pristine condition and with a certain understated beauty of its own. Perched on a hedge behind me, a blackcap bursts into song, its repertoire of uplifting fluted notes serenading chestnut-brown-capped females. I lean back, rest on my elbows and look out over a sun-bathed ancient meadow, knowing that soon it will reveal the purples and pinks of hundreds of green-winged orchids and the sulphur tufts of clover, the prelude to a gentle riot of colour and diversity that will alter and flow throughout the summer months. I share this space with an abundance of life, most of it unseen but still somehow tangible, an intricate web in which I am a fortunate constituent, at least for an hour or so. The sun warms my face. Never has a cheese and pickle sandwich tasted so good.

22nd April

I bought a hammock a few years ago, on a whim. It has a pleasingly curved oak frame and sits in the garden for much of the year like a stranded vessel without a sail. This afternoon, however, there are no pressing tasks to do and the book I have been reading over the past few weeks is only a solid hour or so of quiet time away from being finished. Attaching the canvas using sturdy metal pins slotted into holes at each end of the curve, and placing a pillow behind my head, I settle down in the soporific warmth and begin to read.

Some time later, I am startled out of my slumber by a familiar, repeated refrain. Did a cuckoo just pass over the garden? Stumbling out of the hammock, searching the skies and the field beyond for any sign of the bird, there are only jackdaws, a swallow overhead and a woodpigeon's deep repetitive song. Abruptly woken from a deep sleep, still a bit discombobulated, might I have mistaken the final flurry of a wood pigeon's call for a cuckoo? In a bit of a daze, I calculate that if it was a cuckoo then it was likely heading towards either the gravel pits or the water meadows. I head down to the latter, mainly because it is marginally closer to my house and, at the very least, I might hear or see the curlews. I put on my boots and try to contain my excitement by deciding that it probably was a pigeon. Almost certainly. But just in case.

Rabbits' tails flash for the cover of hedgerows as I pass through a gateway and into the water meadow. Healthy, porous soils have transformed in just a few months a field under water into one cushioned with a rich mosaic of herbs, grasses and sedges taking on fresh growth, carpeting the ground in forty shades of green. Flowering daisies, celandines and dandelions speckle the verdant ridges. In the furrows dull orange and brown tones dominate, denoting stressed vegetation recovering after months of submergence. The golden cups of marsh marigold flow through a few of the furrows, as do pink-washed milk-maids, also known as cuckoo-flowers, so named because their opening buds herald the arrival of the migrant bird. The signs are looking promising.

Lapwings display over the meadow on the far side of the river and a curlew burbles and twirls as it comes in to land. By my boots the flat, arrow-shaped leaves of meadow vetchling link together and run through a few reddened stems of meadow saxifrage, pure white petals just visible, peeking above the sepals, one or two with open flowers. I kneel for a closer look and scan the ground ahead of me. A week or so from now, if the good weather holds, this ridge will be snow white. It was spotting this flower a good while ago that first alerted me to the richness that this meadow holds, and in successive years I have always found something new, whether it be an insect, plant, or just noticing the subtle changes to the mix and abundance of species growing together and apart.

Both the male and female curlew are in the grassland beyond, preening in the sunshine, rather unexpectedly sharing their patch with a male wigeon, the marmalade stripe on its head unmistakable. I had thought that they had long departed. Common terns with long forked tails and sleek black caps follow the course of the river, occasionally pausing to hover with heads bent, searching the waters below.

I start for the adjacent meadow, a part of me distracted, and almost step on an adder's-tongue fern. I could search all afternoon and not spot one. These are plants that you just happen upon. They are far removed from the ferns presently unfurling in the woodland, being constructed of a single undivided waxy frond resembling a tongue sticking out from the turf. This tongue is small and curled in when young, as much shadow as plant, and so you have to pass by at just the right angle to spot one; once the grass takes on the warmth of late spring, they will become almost impossible to find. Its common name actually refers to the stalk that snakes up from the base of the frond. Though very thin and no more than a couple of centimetres long, it is sturdy and will ping back into position if bent by a finger, or a hoof. Evenly spaced dark stripes are just visible at its edges. These are the sporangia, which will later release thousands of spores to be dispersed on the wind. Like the saxifrage, once I get my eye in I see them scattered throughout the turf, and moving into the next meadow it is difficult to look down and not find the fern in quantity; this in a field that was sprayed in the distant past. Growing amongst the ferns there are dark-green crinkle-edged leaves of marsh ragwort, which superficially resembles common ragwort when in flower. Perhaps its presence was the reason for past herbicide use, though livestock will avoid eating it. If the intended aim was to rid the field of the plant, then subsequent decades of sympathetic management have put things right.

I stand and admire the landscape I have become rooted within, at tall two-tone hedgerows, the flat expanse of water meadows flowing into the distance with a winding river. A snapshot of the woodland is just visible on the horizon. Majestic willows line the bankside, with thick alder woodland beyond. A church with no steeple sits on a knoll in the distance, an unchanging sentinel watching over thirty generations of people and wildlife and seasons that have come and gone. A cow bellows in the distance, soon to be turned out with its newborn calf. Skylarks sing above wheat fields ascending to meet the neighbouring village and the hum of the oblivious arterial network beyond. The sun beats down its warmth. Then, for a few seconds, all sound is muted save for a clear, hiccoughing call. The two-note song is repeated a second, third, fourth time and I catch sight of a sleek, streamlined body with curved, pointed wingtips racing towards a bank of shimmering reeds and the scrubby margins of a small island that bisects the river's flow. A jumbled insect cloud flickers in the light. Red kites and buzzards share the thermals high above. The scratchy song of warblers starts up again, and from the top of a gilded willow, the cuckoo calls the year.

 The Cuckoo (Part VI)

My Bonny Cuckoo, I tell thee true
That through the groves I'll rove with you
I'll rove with you until the next spring
And then my cuckoo shall sweetly sing
The ash and the hazel shall morning say
Oh, Bonny Cuckoo, don't go away
Don't go away, but tarry here
And sing for us through all the year
Cuckoo, cuckoo, pray tarry here
And make the spring last all the year

[Traditional]

Acknowledgments

My family's generous acceptance of frequent absences and innumerable hours spent outdoors has always allowed me the time and space to pursue my interests/obsessions. I consider myself a very fortunate man, and try not to take it for granted.

Bill Meek, naturalist par excellence, was kind enough to read an early draft and provide valuable comments on the text, and Simon Leach, taraxacologist extraordinaire, offered much-needed encouragement as I contemplated publication. Long ago, Pete Garner introduced me to the rudimentaries of plant identification, and Alan Barclay offered me my first job in ecology. Their influence, though brief, has been long-lasting, as has the botanical camaraderie of many others over the years, including, but by no means exclusively restricted to, Graham Bellamy, Jon Graham, Franc Hughes, Sarah Hulmes, Dave Mould, Owen Mountford, David Pearman, Claire Pinches, Chris Preston, and Kev Walker.

My nearish-neighbour Carry Akroyd is both a gifted and generous artist, and I'm thankful for her beautiful cover design, the papercuts which illustrate each month, and for her advice whilst this book was in its infancy.

I feel very fortunate to be associated with Merlin Unwin, and I thank Karen, Jo, Joanne, Lydia and Margaret for their skills, enthusiasm and professionalism, and for taking a chance on someone who is not a 'known name'.

I've summarised, hopefully with some degree of accuracy, a few of the exemplary research studies about the cuckoo undertaken by Nick Davis and members of his research team based at the University of Cambridge, who aim to solve complex behavioural puzzles with deceptively simple experimental designs. Thanks to Nick for pointing me towards relevant papers, and for pleasant chats on the Fen.

Lastly, I thank a faithful friend who kept me company on so many of my wanderings, and is still missed on every walk.